Times of Grace

Times of Grace

Spiritual Rhythms of the Year at the University of Notre Dame

Nicholas Ayo, C.S.C.

ROWMAN & LITTLEFIELD PUBLISHERS, INC.

Lanham • Boulder • New York • Toronto • Oxford

ROWMAN & LITTLEFIELD PUBLISHERS, INC.

Published in the United States of America
by Rowman & Littlefield Publishers, Inc.
A wholly owned subsidary of The Rowman & Littlefield Publishing
Group, Inc.
4501 Forbes Boulevard, Suite 200, Lanham, Maryland 20706
www.rowmanlittlefield.com

PO Box 317
Oxford
OX2 9RU, UK

British Library Cataloguing in Publication Information Available

Library of Congress Cataloging-in-Publication Data

Ayo, Nicholas.
      Times of grace : spiritual rhythms of the year at the University of
   Notre Dame / Nicholas Ayo.
      p. cm.
   ISBN 0-7425-3394-8 (cloth : alk. paper)
   1. Meditations. 2. University of Notre Dame. I. Title.

BX2182.3.A96 2004
242'.2—dc22   2003015647

Printed in the United States of America

♾ ™ The paper used in this publication meets the minimum require-
ments of American National Standard for Information Sciences—
Permanence of Paper for Printed Library Materials, ANSI/NISO
Z39.48-1992.

Dedicated to Emil T. Hofman
Professor Emeritus of Chemistry
Dean of First-Year Studies at Notre Dame

In the "Wall of Honor" corridor in the Main Building of the University of Notre Dame, a small selection of exceptionally charismatic men and women, whose dedication and giftedness embodied in the university the pursuit of excellence, is honored with an engraved plaque displaying their profile and a few words about their contribution over the years to Notre Dame.

Of Professor Emil T. Hofman, the plaque reads:

Respected by his colleagues, feared for his quizzes by those enrolled in his general chemistry course, and loved by more than 32,000 University alumni he taught during his career, Hofman also served as dean of the Freshman Year of Studies, reorganizing the first-year curriculum, introducing a nationally celebrated counseling program, and greatly reducing freshman class attrition.

Contents

 **Autumn**

Winter

Spring

Summer

Foreword

FOR THE TENS of thousands of pilgrims, visitors, and fans who converge on Notre Dame each year, the campus is a place with many favorite spots that personalize every journey. For some, it is a years-long routine that precedes and follows football games and includes a steak sandwich at the Knights of Columbus, a visit to the Grotto, and Mass at the Basilica. For the first-time visitors, it may be trying to catch on film as many angles of the Golden Dome as possible, and the many other venues that are a source of inspiration. For high school juniors and seniors visiting with their parents the campus which might one day be theirs, the draw lies in imagining what it would be like to call Notre Dame their home.

Often it is a special spot, perhaps the Grotto, or a view of campus from across the lake, or a hall chapel where a young couple worshiped on many Sunday nights, or the place where a young man proposes to the woman who becomes his fiancée. Nicholas Ayo's *Signs of Grace* captured beautifully the scores of places on campus that mean so much to so many people who come from every walk of life and make Notre Dame a place of national pilgrimage. And for faculty, staff, and students who have read the book, *Signs of Grace* quickly became a source of prayer and meditation which spoke to their hearts about why so many different places on campus have come to mean so much to them.

In *Times of Grace*, Father Ayo produces a sequel of a kind, which introduces profound reflections on the different moments and events that are part of the academic year. He shares his own deep spiritual insights into what might too often pass as traditionally scheduled events and teases out of them their deeper meaning and relationship to everyday spiritual growth. Combining a poet's sensitivity, a spiritual writer's grace, and a person of letter's eloquence, Father Ayo produces yet another gem well worth reading over and over again.

Times of Grace gives words to sentiments and feelings many members of the Notre Dame community will identify with immediately, as the book draws insights out of ordinary events and captures the essence of the extraordinary things that take place on campus each year. *Times of Grace* is an unusual companion book to *Signs of Grace* (Places of Grace), which complements it well and leads us to a deeper understanding of how God can speak to us through the ordinary events of a year and lead us to deepen our relationship with God. This book captures in a remarkable way *the Spiritual Rhythms of the Year at the University of Notre Dame.*

Richard V. Warner, C.S.C.
Director of Campus Ministry
University of Notre Dame

Prologue

SIGNS OF GRACE, the predecessor of this book, was written with an eye to places on the campus that might appear ordinary but, when dwelled upon with attention, become meditations on the spiritual suggestiveness of the places we have known and loved in our lives and especially on this campus. *Times of Grace* was written with an eye to the events on the campus that might appear ordinary but, like the campus places, are more than ordinary. Beginning with the opening of the academic year at the end of summer, the reflections in this book follow the calendar year and the liturgical year at Notre Dame. Events that touch deeply the life of the campus are noticed, and some spiritual implications teased out. We would live a spiritual life at Notre Dame, and indeed one hopes all people everywhere would do so. This book is a soulful collection of appreciative moments during one year on the campus of the University of Notre Dame. It is meant to be evocative. My thoughts need not be the reader's, but my thoughts I hope will encourage the reader to cultivate his or her own and not to discount the wonder of everyday events—truly times of grace.

So rarely are we attentive to what is going on in our hearts and souls as the times of our days unfold. We are lulled to sleep by habit and by a culture of future shock squared. We move so fast. We multitask. We less and less attend, and thus we do not pray always, and then we are lonely inside. "Attention is the natural prayer of the soul," says one philosopher. To attend, to pay attention to whatever comes along in our days, can be a habitual prayer. The child who examines a bug or watches the moon with awe lives that attentive life that is contemplative prayer. We have but to slow down, even stop, and pay attention to what is happening in this our moment. Painters are artists who can see what is there in its fullness. Most of us are not really looking at all. We do not notice what the painter notices. We fail to see the subtleties of light and shadow. So much is lost on us because we are often preoccupied with regrets about the past and fears about the future. We are project driven. To waste time in just looking, or just listening, or just breathing in and out in wonder that we are alive, becomes a rare use of our time. Why anything? How wonderful everything! Those reflections raise the mind and heart to God, who is Creator and whose providence gifts us with this time and this space. "So, whether you eat or drink, or whatever you do, do everything for the glory of God" (1 Cor 10:31).[1]

The morning after the twin World Trade Center towers in New York City collapsed, I walked along a path aside the Main Building at the University of Notre Dame to early mass in the crypt. I thought of the summer of 1879, when that building, which then was the whole university—classrooms, dormitories, dining, and administration—burned to the ground. They had no bulldozers and no cranes, but by an enormous effort, the whole community cleared the rubble

---

1. I have quoted from the New Revised Standard Version of the Bible throughout this volume.

and built a new and bigger university building in a few months and in time to open school in September. No doubt not every detail was finished, but they had a roof over their heads. I recall the words of the founder of the university, who said that he thought God was telling him in this tragedy that he had built too small and that Notre Dame should now become a bigger and better university. I thought to myself, What would Father Sorin say today? Perhaps he would suggest we rebuild the twin towers of world commerce bigger and better. Let us raise up a third tower, one devoted to the concerns of the world of people whose hopes and desires for a better life have yet to be achieved. Let us build a tower to one world, a world of equal justice and peace, a world where there is food and water and a good life for everyone. I am not saying the troubles of the disadvantaged nations of the world are all the fault of our country. I am not saying that their troubles are not in part their own fault. I am saying that we could build a bigger and better world. And we would make more friends than enemies, though I do not say we will ever overcome evil altogether in this world. Not all the evil of the world, however, is in the Third World, and not all the innocence of the world is in our First World. We are always part of the whole world, part of its agonies and part of its ecstasies. We are a generous people, but we are not always focused on the implications of our way of life. We could do better in bringing about one world, where everyone is recognized and loved as a child of God.

On the campus of the university, classes were canceled on that September 11, and the day became a day of prayer. I had met my first class early in the morning, before the official announcement, and tried to say something intelligible in the midst of an unfolding chaos. There was a sad pall over the room. One student was crying aloud. We all were crying on the inside. Not long into words we disbanded to grieve, each in our own way with whomever we most could hold on to. In the afternoon, mass was celebrated on the grass of the central mall. Thousands crowded about on all sides. The president of the university spoke of how we should try to channel our pain into efforts to solve the problems facing our country. Even in dire situations, we are people of peace and people of forgiveness. We prayed for those injured or killed; we prayed for strength for ourselves in the days to come as the news worsened. At the end we sang the alma mater, which concludes, "Proudly in the heavens gleams thy gold and blue." And the golden dome of the university did stand tall and bright in the cloudless summer blue skies. I thought of the towers gleaming in the smoke and fire, and the contrast seemed unbearable.

On the way back down the sidewalk to the Knights of Columbus building (the old post office of the university), where we vested for the mass, I noticed a child wiggling and crying in its mother's arms. It was trying to reach the water cups on the tables set up to provide drinking water for the crowds. I thought, "The child wants only to play with the cups and with the water." And then I thought of all the children in so many places around the world who might be crying to drink clean water and to eat enough food. We can and must do more for them if ever the world is to know justice, and without justice we shall never know peace. Education, both intellectual and spiritual, has a crucial role to play in this new world, and the spiritual life of the campus of Notre Dame is integral to an education at this Catholic university. This book speaks of that spiritual life over an academic year.

Acknowledgments

 MANY PEOPLE have generously assisted me in this endeavor. In particular I am thankful to Alida Ayo Macor; Father Leonard Banas, C.S.C.; Kathleen Macor Karras; Emil Hofman; and my student assistant, Sheila Payne. As readers of the typescript in its developmental stages, they suggested improvements and kindly noticed shortcomings. James Langford has encouraged me as a writer for many years, and his assistance as an editor for Rowman & Littlefield made possible the publication of the predecessor to this book, *Signs of Grace*, in 2001. Kathie McGowan and several of the staff of the book department of the Notre Dame Bookstore have supported my previous writings with publicity and encouragement. Cheryl Reed assisted me with her computer expertise. Richard Warner, C.S.C., and Don McNeill, C.S.C., deserve my gratitude for timely assistance, each in his own way. The support of the members of the Congregation of Holy Cross, as well as the faculty and students of the Program of Liberal Studies and the University of Notre Dame, is so constant as to be hardly noticed, but it is not taken for granted. I remain grateful and beholden to all these people and others unmentioned, whose contributions I may have forgotten or overlooked. "No man is an island" is a wisdom well understood by authors.

"Running in Church," a poem by Annie Finch, is reprinted with permission from *Eve: Poems by Annie Finch* (Ashland, Oreg.: Story Line Press, 1997), 2.

Lyrics for the song "Christ Has No Body Now but Yours," by Steven C. Warner, copyright © 2003, World Library Publications (All Rights Reserved). Phone (800) 566–6150. Reprinted with permission.

Throughout the book I have quoted from the New Revised Standard Version of the Bible.

Autumn

Morning Prayer

First Day of Class

Opening Mass of the Academic Year

Our Lady, Seat of Wisdom

Vow Profession Day

Dorm Sunday Night Mass

Saint Edward

All Saints' Day

Veterans Day

Saint Elizabeth of Hungary

Christ the King

Morning Prayer: Every Day

 "FIRST THINGS FIRST" is a popular saying that reminds us to prioritize the hours of our all-too-busy days. To turn to God at the first moment we awake enables us to re-create our world. Overnight we forget that our God holds the whole world in the palm of his hand, and even if a mother should forget her child, our God will never forget us. "See, I have inscribed you on the palms of my hands" (Is 49:16). Morning prayer reconstitutes our place in God's world. We are born again from the unconscious darkness of sleep. I would prefer to pray morning prayer out of doors, summer or winter, as the sunrise colors a lightly clouded sky from horizon to horizon. The world is created anew with the coming of the dawning light. The heavens seem the appropriate church to praise the creation of a new day.

When I was a boy in Catholic grammar school taught by Benedictine sisters, we were urged to say the morning offering first thing. Work that is done with a prayer is more sacred work. Life that is lived with a prayer is more spiritual life. A day that is begun without bringing God to mind and offering ourselves in God's service runs the risk of being a day empty of deeper meaning. In Luke's Gospel, Jesus prays often, and always before important events in his life, such as the choosing of his disciples. Frequently he prayed alone during the night because the daytime was filled with the crowds pressing upon him on all sides for his healing touch. When Mother Teresa was asked if she became discouraged at the magnitude of the problem of the poor and the abandoned on the streets of Calcutta, she is reported to have said that God asks only that we take care of God's people, these our brothers and our sisters. The outcome of our labor is in God's hands. We do not need to succeed; we need only to care. God "will prosper the work of our hands" (Ps 90:17). And Mother Teresa began her workday always with a long time of morning prayer.

Morning mass seems to me an ideal morning offering. It is a Eucharistic prayer that brings our body and soul to the altar as bread and wine to be changed into the body of Christ ministering in this world to the body of Christ in our daily routine. The students in the residence halls of Notre Dame favor evening masses, and especially on Sundays. I suppose one might consider the evening hour their morning hour, for night has been changed into day in the lives of college students. I can imagine it is easier to study in the night, when the distractions of the day outside one's window are masked by the darkness. And yet, I know our waking hours, whenever they may be, if lived without prayer to recognize God's grace working in us, will be diminished time. When what we say, think, and do is done for Christ and in Christ, our humble everyday takes on a hidden melody. We hum along a love song of the love God has given us and of our moment to stand for him in this place, and we pass along that love to those whose lives we touch. "Be well, do good work, stay in touch" is how Garrison Keillor ends his engaging *Writer's Almanac.*

But, poignant as his aphoristic advice remains, I think I would rather conclude the morning offering of our lives with the doxology of the liturgy: "Through him, with him, and in him is to you almighty Father all honor and glory forever and ever. Amen."

In this book of campus meditations, I think of the first things in the lives of the students at the University of Notre Dame. I will suggest that it is here on this campus that our students make many of their first independent decisions and claim their own judgment. Of course, I know that our students have lived rich lives before they came here. They have made choices, including a significant one to attend Notre Dame, and they have known the sacraments of the Church for a long time. What is different in college years is this: One is no longer in one's home with one's family. One is on one's own as never before. The university may thus become an alma mater, a nourishing and caring mother, just as mother earth or "holy mother church," and one's college friends may be closer than a brother or sister who is much older or much younger. Here and now one must sink or swim on one's own. There are many discoveries in these precious years balanced exquisitely between childhood innocence and adult responsibility. There are many decisions that were never so deliberately made and owned from the inside out. In Tolstoy's *War and Peace*, Natasha exclaims during a Christmas nighttime sleigh ride that she might never be as happy again. Engaged to be married and yet still living at home, she is old enough to be on her own and still young enough to be protected. College years, it seems to me, reveal the maturity of adulthood and the playfulness of childhood in a delicate balance. One has a foot in both camps, and perhaps never again can one be quite so serious and quite so silly and at the same time.

First Day of Class: Late August

TEACHERS BEGIN a new class in a new semester with new and unknown students. Nine months and two semesters later, we deliver the finished product of this academic year, a gestation reminiscent of the patient waiting a woman experiences in bringing forth the child of her body. We labor to give birth to education in the young and to the maturation of their mind, heart, and soul. And when graduation day for the seniors comes, one knows that the task is over, whatever the outcome. For better or for worse, the slate is wiped clean, and one will begin all over in innocence after the summer's pause.

Let us talk about how the academic year begins with the first day of class and in particular how it might feel for the teachers as well as for students. At the beginning of the semester, when the students do not know each other, they come to class with the hesitancy and feared humiliation of saying something stupid. First-year students especially need encouragement. I take their pictures on the first day with a Polaroid camera and give them a color-copy sheet with all their photos and names. We rehearse their names on the first day, and thereafter I give surprise "quizzes" throughout the semester. So and so, please name all the women in the class. So and so, please name all the men. I ask first names one week and first and last names another week. By midterm most of the students can spontaneously name everyone. To name is to respect in a special way. I have watched students become friends because there was a name basis for a relationship.

On the first day of class I look the students over with an eye to understanding them, but in reality they are looking me over with an eye to figuring me out. Where else on earth does one stand before a group of people and have them listen mainly, if not exclusively, to your one person for forty-plus hours? They know your every mannerism. They read your values by how you treat their questions and how you regard the less gifted students as well as the gifted ones. They have long antennae set to pick up signals of unfairness and favoritism. They know when you are unprepared, when you are bluffing an answer you do not fully comprehend, and when you are troubled by what they say and do. Most of all, they have an infectious participation in your excitement and your love for your words and for the truth of your profession. They want so much to be given the simple truth. Education can be so confusing. Sometimes what is said in one discipline seems to be undone by what is claimed in another classroom. Students yearn for someone who shares with them the task of synthesis and integration. They are trying to find out more deeply who they are, what they believe, and what they should do. What I am in front of them is memorable, even if what I say will soon be forgotten. In the end they will forget most everything I say. Only one-liners that are humorous or outrageous seem to be remembered, and even then in distortion. But students do not forget the heart and soul of their teacher if what was taught was invested with insight and personal care for them.

On the first day of class, my fears of teaching come to the fore. At first I seem to have nothing to say to these students, and in the next moment I have everything to say and not world enough or time to say the half of it. Perhaps teachers (and students) relive the first day of first-grade class, when we abandoned the security of home and familiar playmates to confront a room full of equals whose regard we had not earned and a teacher whose conduct, for better or for worse, we could only imagine. I remember my first homework assignment at age five. We were to write out the alphabet, and I turned in a cursive alphabet when the teacher expected a print alphabet. Cursive was more advanced learning, but what I remember to this day was the wrongness. On my first day in a college class at Notre Dame, I remember an older and distinguished professor by the name of John Frederick asking us what made a good dictionary. I had no answer, but I will never forget his answer. A dictionary with supplemental pictures in the margins would be best, he thought, because a picture was worth a thousand words.

On the first day of class at Notre Dame, no one has momentum, and typically teachers give a *lectio brevis*, a short opening and introductory class, designed as much to accommodate those who have yet to settle their course registration or other logistical problems as it is intended to allow for a gradual coming to speed. I used to worry about being anxious on the first day of class, until I recognized that my students were also preoccupied, and indeed perhaps more so after a summer away from campus than am I, living on campus. I try to remember on the first day that my task is not to make my students like me but rather to help them to know me by giving of myself and by teaching them something true and well explained. And then they may even come to love me. To teach young students remains an awesome privilege, a day-by-day challenge rarely met to one's satisfaction. Often I leave class feeling that I said too much or too little. One wants to give, but one wants the students to give. On the first day of class, that adventure begins always unknown—each moment a first time, never to be repeated.

Opening Mass of the Academic Year

 SUNDAY MASS is celebrated for the first-year students upon their arrival at Notre Dame. That mass welcomes the new students and their parents, family, and friends who escorted them and their multifarious gear to the campus, where amid rain or heat or both, a population that could qualify as a small city tries all at once to move into a new home. This Sunday morning mass is a farewell-and-good-bye (God be with ye) moment because the temptation is to linger, and the best thing the family can do for their beloved daughter or son now is to head back home. I give out Eucharistic communion to long lines winding down from the attic of the basketball arena seats, and I see a sea of gold rings on the hands outstretched as a cushion for the body of Jesus, our bread of life, to rest upon. I see the years of fidelity to wife or to husband, the years of devotion as mother or father to their child now praying with them as a new student at Notre Dame. The cantor at this mass one year had been a student of mine the preceding year. I had not known she sang so beautifully. One of the readers at the mass that year had been my student some years before, and he was now a graduate student in the Master of Divinity program at Notre Dame. I see them as our family now. I think of the parents in front of me who remember their child as the tiny helpless infant they once held in their hands and who now stands at their side, proud to begin a college education. How many stories of faith, devotion, and heroism brought us to this day.

The opening mass of the academic year was celebrated for many years in the Basilica of the Sacred Heart on a Sunday morning in the middle of September. There was room for the faculty and some of the accustomed Sunday worshipers, but there was no room for the student body or the university staff and their families. The opening mass became a mass for the Notre Dame faculty alone, and the homily was given by the provost and addressed to the university faculty in attendance. More recently the opening mass has taken place in the Joyce Convocation Center in the late afternoon of the very first day of classes in the autumn semester. The several student choirs proclaim a clear awareness that this mass is for the whole university community, faculty and families, staff members and families, and the Notre Dame students one and all. Notre Dame is our university, and the Eucharistic liturgy especially reveals our community.

At the opening mass of the school year, now celebrated in the basketball arena of the Joyce Convocation Center, the students fill half the amphitheater, and the priests, vested in red chasubles for a mass of the Holy Spirit, fill the altar platform. Many of the faculty of the university attend in cap and gown, and the rectors of the residence halls distribute communion to the student body, whom they will continue to serve day and night throughout the academic year. Catholics believe the bread and wine become the body and blood of Jesus, and we communicants are the grains of wheat and grapes of wine. Students and faculty and staff, we the family of Notre Dame, we the human race, we become the body of Christ. We become the offering, and we are transformed into the body of Christ. I think with Annie Dillard that we take the awesome quality of the Eucharist too much for granted. As she so bravely says: "It is madness to wear ladies' straw hats and velvet hats to church; we should all be wearing crash helmets. Ushers should issue life preservers and signal flares; they should lash us to our pews. For the sleeping god may wake someday and take offense, or the waking god may draw us out to where we can never return."[1]

To give communion to many thousands in that arena takes some time. Becoming the body of Christ takes time. Be patient, my soul. God has boundless time. Planet earth is four billion years old, and if the time of our world were calendared into one year, human beings would have appeared at nine in the evening of December 31. Humanity is only 150,000 years old, and we have not seen what we may yet become. Even now we are being given eternal life.

After the opening mass, the congregation is served a cookout buffet supper on DeBartolo Quad. Twilight comes early in late August, and the fireworks begin in the gathering darkness. The display of sound and light seems each year to grow more spectacular. The stars seem to be falling, just as the world coming into its glory is imagined in the Gospel of Mark: "And the stars will be falling from heaven, and the powers in the heavens will be shaken. Then they will see 'the Son

1. *Teaching a Stone to Talk* (New York: HarperCollins, 1983; HarperPerennial, 1992), 52–53.

of Man coming in clouds' with great power and glory. Then he will send out the angels, and gather his elect from the four winds, from the ends of the earth to the ends of heaven" (13:25–27). So beautiful these bursts of color in the black velvet sky, so beautiful the final hoped-for consummation of the world. We should not be afraid. With the early Christians, we would say, "Amen. Come, Lord Jesus!" (Rv 22:20). Though it may take a world of time to become a new heaven and new earth, though it may take all of time to become fully the body of Christ, yet we believe such an evening glory has been promised in the end. We believe that the body of Christ has well begun the transformation of the world. We believe that, full of hope, we have begun the academic year at the University of Notre Dame in the continuing pursuit of the true, the good, and the beautiful—the embodiment of God in this our universe.

Our Lady,
Seat of Wisdom[2]

I OFTEN WANDER early in the morning in front of Corby Hall, where I reside, with coffee cup in hand while enjoying a contemplative mood. Joggers pass me by on the sidewalk, and one apologized one day for having no coins for my cup. With eyes wide open to whatever might appear and with ears attentive to the sounds of campus life, I watch the sun rise. This morning I hear only the faraway rumble of the diesel locomotives pulling freight through the heart of South Bend and the humming of window air conditioners. Birds at times pierce that background with their cries. A drop of dew on a hibiscus flower on an old bush by the side of the road near Sorin Hall seems a diamond in the rough. The intricate branches and needles of the evergreens overwhelm one's capacity to notice, much less remember. We would be satisfied with so much less, as Annie Dillard said so well.[3] And then, I think, why should there be anything at all? And what

2. The Nativity of the Blessed Virgin Mary.
3. Annie Dillard, *Pilgrim at Tinker Creek* (New York: HarperPerennial, 1998).

is this beautiful and sometimes sad world's ultimate source and fulfilling destiny? We all seek a unified vision of this world and our life. Our studies should hang together in a uni-versity, which should never be a multi-versity.

There are those who think a Catholic university is an oxymoron,[4] a contradiction in terms, such as "hot ice" or "cold fire." If Notre Dame is truly a university, it cannot be a church; if a church, it cannot be a university. If open to all truth, it cannot be Catholic; if Catholic, it cannot be open. Let us propose that a Catholic university should be seen as a work in progress. We may not have yet achieved a Catholic university at its full potential. The daring marriage of faith and reason has yet to be brought to its fulfillment. Faith needs reason to investigate what the words mean that we use to share the revelation of religion. Reason needs faith to expand its reach and to recognize its ultimate purpose. We walk with two legs, our weight on one leg and then the other. Scissors will cut only when both blades come together. So faith and reason, Catholic and university, God and humankind belong together. When we see with binocular vision, there is depth of field and a third dimension that we do not enjoy if we see with only one eye. Jesus is Lord of heaven and earth, and Jesus is one of us in his humanity. Thus we begin an inner voyage to the stars when we begin an academic year with such a frame of mind and heart. We bring all of it and all of us to our

---

4. Actually, "Catholic university" is not an oxymoron, as some skeptics would claim, but rather a pleonasm. A pleonasm is a redundancy, like "round sphere." "Catholic," in its etymology, means universal, and a Catholic university is a universal university. In short, the pursuit of truth in a Catholic university should be the pursuit of the universal truth of the universe, and mindful most of all of its one Creator.

Eucharist on opening day of class in order to remind ourselves that in Jesus Christ we acknowledge that the human and divine have become entwined. The world's human business is now ever God's divine business, for divinity has been embodied in our humanity—the Word made flesh.

Named after the thirteenth president of the University of Notre Dame, Malloy Hall houses the entire department of philosophy and the department of theology. The right-angle wings embrace in the building's two arms the chapel of Our Lady, Seat of Wisdom. The architectural medium is the message, for a Catholic university is nothing if not the integration of faith and reason, of theology and philosophy, of that world of eternity and this world of time, of the Creator and the creation. No easy marriage guaranteed, no dance of two partners without some stepping on each other's toes, no easy amalgamation. As one professor at the university quipped of the new building's residential combination of philosophy and theology: "not yet a marriage but at least a wary cohabitation." Truly we live in mystery, as did Mary, Seat of Wisdom. The Gospel of Luke twice tells us that "Mary treasured all these words and pondered them in her heart" (2:19 and 2:51). She knew so little of this child on her lap, who had created her from nothing and yet was dependent on her for everything.

The bas-relief mural sculpted by Father James Flanigan, C.S.C., on the outer wall of the chapel depicts a sturdy and determined young mother seated with her child centered on her lap and facing the world. She is Mary, Seat of Wisdom. Mary, the Mother of God, holds the first chair in philosophy and in theology. The hand of her divine Son rests in her hand and his body rests on her lap as it nested in her before he was born. Both their hands are raised in a blessing given to the whole world. The Son of God was incarnate in Mary, and thereby the life of God was enfleshed in the life of the whole world. Divine grace was embodied in our human mind and heart. This mural of Mary as Seat of Wisdom is contained in an egg-shaped frame that shows the sky above her and the waters beneath her. The motto of the University of Notre Dame proclaims the Madonna "our life, our sweetness, and our hope" (*Vita, Dulcedo, Spes* in Latin),[5] and it is inscribed on the cover of the book the child Jesus holds on his lap. Jesus, the wisdom of God made human in the child on Mary's lap, proclaims Mary the Mother of God and the Seat of Wisdom, human and divine.

---

5. The Notre Dame motto is taken from the medieval hymn "Salve Regina."

Vow Profession Day: Early September

RARELY IS THERE a football game on the very first weekend of the autumn semester, and were there such an opening of the season, the Basilica event described below would be postponed. Usually on the first Saturday of the fall semester at the University of Notre Dame, the custom has been to celebrate the final public profession of the young men, most of them Notre Dame graduates, who this year choose to give their life to God and the service of the Church in the Congregation of Holy Cross. They publicly consecrate their life to God much as do all Christians in their sacrament of baptism. The profession of the religious vows of poverty, chastity, and obedience but heightens and focuses the self-giving that is the essence of the Christian life in imitation of him who said, "I am the way and the truth and the life" (Jn 14:6). With lyrics so apropos to the moment, we sing:

> Christ has no body now but yours, no hands but yours. Here on this earth, yours is the work, to serve with the joy of compassion. No hands but yours to heal the

wounded world, no hands but yours to soothe all suffering, no touch but yours to bind the broken dreams
of the people of God.[6]

In the *Constitutions of the Congregation of Holy Cross*, we find
a succinct commentary on the meaning of the vowed religious life:

We profess vows for the sake of the mission of Jesus.
In consecrated celibacy we wish to love with the
freedom, openness, and availability that can be recognized as a sign of the kingdom. In consecrated
poverty we seek to share the lot of the poor and to
unite in their cause, trusting in the Lord as provider.
In consecrated obedience we join with our brothers
in community and with the whole church in the
search for God's will. We do not imagine that those
who commit themselves in other ways to the following of Jesus are thereby hindered in their service
of neighbor. On the contrary, we find in them willing and complementary partners in shared mission.
We want our vows, faithfully lived, to be witness and
call to them as their commitments, faithfully lived,
are witness and call to us (5:44).

On this occasion the Basilica is filled to capacity. Several
of these young men spent some previous years in service to the
neighboring parishes or to the campus, and the people who

---

6. Steven C. Warner, "Christ Has No Body Now but Yours," based
on a prayer of Teresa of Avila (Schiller Park, Ill: World Library
Publications, 2003). All rights reserved.

received their care are grateful. They admire what these young men are today wanting to do. We all know that marriage is an adventure. The conjoining of a man and woman and of their families endeavors to raise up a new family of children. Their lives will interact with many others in a wider world and expand in concentric circles like the ripples radiating from a single stone dropped in the water. Marriage to the Church endeavors to devote a lifetime of loving service of the people of God. Such a vocation might well preclude a focus upon one family and its recurrent demands in order to be available to whomever or whatever, whenever and wherever the providence of God and the ecclesial community in its discernment wishes to send the religious brother or sister. Church weddings are enthusiastic. After the profession of vows at the foot of the altar, the congregation in the Basilica breaks into exuberant and prolonged applause. And so have I when in attendance in the sanctuary as a member of the Congregation of Holy Cross and a member of the wedding party.

Applause in church still strikes me awkwardly. I was brought up only to whisper in church. My first reaction is a bit of a shock. What is going on? Then, I think nostalgically how good I would have felt had someone applauded when I walked down the aisle in my profession to God in the vowed community of Holy Cross. It just was not done in those days. We were told that the community did us a favor to accept us, and not that we did them a favor to join them. It was a different church world, and I do not wish to fault anyone in that era. We are all children of our times, and I believe with all my heart that we all are doing the best we can, given our education and our many wounds, both received and given. Then I think that perhaps we ought not to applaud people only at the beginning of their dedication. Profession Day is short; life is long. Many church marriages end in divorce, and many professed religious abandon their springtime commitment some years into the summer heat. How strange is applause given to young men who have hardly begun to fight. I never heard of baseball players applauding rookies. They disdain them, and they wait to see if the hotshots of the minor leagues can cut it in the majors. Bonuses they may rake in, but not the kind of prolonged and enthusiastic applause I hear resounding in the Gothic echoes of Sacred Heart Basilica on this autumn afternoon of Profession Day. How strange the applause, so full of affection and on the verge of tears. Are we applauding these men, or are we applauding what they want to do, what we all in our heart of hearts want to do, what we so admire—to "love the Lord your God with all your heart, and with all your soul, and with all your mind, and with all your strength" (Mk 12:30)? Do they stand in for us, and are we applauding their courage to stand up and say they will put their public lives where our hearts secretly reside? Why we extend all this applause lingers in the back of my mind long after the church has emptied of its crowds.

From where I sit in the sanctuary, I can see the faces of the student choir members singing in the balcony loft. The miracle fingers of the organist are seen in my imagination. Harmony beyond comprehension overwhelms me. To describe them as angelic voices would seem to be no exaggeration. My eyes stray to the faces of the beautiful young women arranged artfully among the choir. When I see them applauding with such joyful enthusiasm, again I am thoughtful. I would have thought they might look upon these young men as potential companions in marriage and resent the decision to decline womanly beauty, presence, and gift of fresh eggs and sweet milk that gives life to the world. But they applaud all the louder, it seems to me.

In the end, who and what are we applauding? Not accomplishment primarily, perhaps courage and generosity, but surely the grace of God. In the end, I think the applause should be understood as applause for God, whose great work in these men has been professed in our midst. God in them is applauded. They have given reception to God's grace, and even that reception, while a decision of their freedom, is yet always also the gift of God's grace. All is gift; all is grace. Now that is something to applaud loudly forever.

Dorm Sunday Night Mass

THERE IS A PIECE of Notre Dame life that visitors almost never share. They may hear about it, but they have not seen it. They may wonder about it, but they have not enjoyed it. When students leave Notre Dame in the summer or graduate in their glory, they miss campus life very much, nor can they easily find the like. A dorm chapel mass late on Sunday evening with those one lives with day in and day out remains unique. Never again in our graduates' lives will so many who share so much worship so often and so well side by side. They come at the very last minute piling down the staircases and into their own chapel within each of the residence halls at Notre Dame. I often wonder, just minutes before we are to begin the Eucharistic liturgy, if anyone is going to show up, but I think quartz watches and groupthink deliver the whole synchronized community on the dot. Supper is by now only a memory, and typical Sunday evening study hours have been well invested. Mass in the late evening provides a break, and it punctuates the weekend with a formal closing and begins the new week much as a morning mass begins the new day. And they do come. Not everyone comes, of course, but the turnout in a residence hall at Notre Dame confirms one's faith. They come to be all together with those they live closely with in their dorm corridors. Some come with their boyfriend or girlfriend from another dorm. Others come to this or that dorm for the music, or for the sermon, or for a gathering of their close friends. Some come for Jesus alone. And all come aware that the mass is special.

If you ask college students about the "real presence" of Jesus in the Eucharistic bread, they may not know what you are asking. The old controversy about real or symbolic presence in the Eucharist is not their quarrel, and the theology of transubstantiation presupposes a philosophy and theology not all of them have encountered. But today's students know what we all know from the days of our first communion. This bread is special. This bread is our bread of life, "taken, blessed, broken, and given" to us by the Lord Jesus, who gave his body and blood to us in his Last Supper, now our Lord's Supper, to which we have been invited.

The students come to a dorm Sunday mass in casual dress. They may come in their slippers. They know each other, and they are at home as well as in the chapel. For the first time in their lives, many of them are at home in the church. The kiss of peace becomes more hugs than handshakes and often goes on and on. I recall myself celebrating the Eucharist with the Pangborn Phoxes, the Knott Angels (later changed into a men's dorm and renamed Knott Juggernauts),[7] the Howard Ducks, the Badin Bullfrogs (a strange name for a women's

7. Personalized license plates are screened for antisocial innuendo and salacious humor, and so are Notre Dame Bookstore basketball team names and residence hall mascot names. Knott Angels wanted to become Knott Beavers, and you do not want to know why.

dorm),[8] the Wild Women of Walsh Hall, the Men of Morrissey Manor, the Stanford Griffins, and the Carroll Vermin. These good folks are our Notre Dame students, these men and women are the people of God, these young adults are the future of America, and these soon-to-be-graduates are the hope of the world. It is their springtime—no winter in its limitations or summer in its exhaustions—all blossom and beauty, a pure and undefiled sacrifice offered to God above. This is the body of Christ, and "how happy we are to be invited to this supper," at which we are served the "bread of life."

I know we Catholics cherish the presence of Jesus in the tabernacle, and yet I know that "real presence" is no theology of God in a box. God is in us. We are the tabernacle of the indwelling of God. We eat the bread that becomes us. We are the living stones that make the church that truly contains the living God. We could follow each other with a vigil light, for we are "temples of the Holy Spirit," as Paul claims (see 1 Cor 3:16–17 and 6:19). I look out on the student community gathered for a late Sunday evening dorm mass, and I see why Jesus loves them so. I could light a candle for them at that moment, not just in the Grotto, but a sanctuary lamp to remind them that they are sacred and beloved of God, whose love for them is boundless. May their goodness shine, for they are becoming the light of the world. "A city built on a hill cannot be hid. . . . Let your light shine before others, so that they may see your good works and give glory to your Father in heaven" (Mt 5:14, 16). Father Theodore M. Hesburgh's words when he was president of the university come to mind at moments like this, when the students are revealed in the

---

8. Bullfrogs can be either male or female.

spiritual beauty God has bestowed on them. Notre Dame students are the best students in the world, he would say, even if they do not always behave. And they do not always behave well. And yet, we love them so.

At the end of mass, announcements are made to the community. One night in Walsh Hall they covered a wide territory: "A Life Uncommon," a support group for women that dealt with issues touching particularly their own gender, would meet at such and such. A talk on how to enjoy the strategy of a football game would be given, and the Notre Dame Leprechaun would be present. Time still left to sign up for the Center for Social Concerns Urban Plunge opportunities over fall break. An Asian fashion show open to all fashions seeks participants. A memorial mass for a former member of Walsh Hall. Still places available for the first-year students' retreat weekend approaching, and also an opportunity for the upcoming Notre Dame Encounter retreat weekend. The all-campus memorial mass on September 11, the first annual remembrance of the New York City terrorist attack, would take place on the quad before the reflecting pool of the Hesburgh Memorial Library. And then we conclude our liturgy with these words: "Let us go in peace to love and serve the Lord in each other."

Saint Edward:
October 13

EDWARD SORIN was a great pioneer of Catholic faith in North America and the founder of a great university, which he had hardly planned to develop in quite such a focused and elaborate way. Edward Sorin was a missionary French priest and not an American Socrates. He wanted to educate the illiterate and promote the faith of the baptized and the converted. He had few doubts about what was needed for a basic education. As time passed and the complexity of higher education impinged upon Notre Dame, Father Sorin left the detailed decisions to others more qualified.

Edward Sorin was not a saint who would ever be canonized, but he might have been had he lived in the days of his patron saint, King Edward, the Saxon king of England just prior to the Norman invasion of England in 1066. King Edward, divided between Norman and English constituencies, would have understood the problem of French and American divergent loyalties and expectations that Edward Sorin would struggle with throughout his lifetime at Notre Dame. Saint King Edward, "the Confessor," defended the church even amid the vicissitudes of political intrigues inevitable in the ways of the world. One could say the same of the university founder, Edward Sorin. In the masterful biography of Edward Sorin completed at the turn of the century by Marvin O'Connell, one recognizes the dilemmas, ambiguities, and compromises required of any "king" in Indiana. Despite the conflicts of his situation, Edward Sorin was a religious man and a man of faith expressed in action. One way or other, all of us at Notre Dame must also confess our "faith," enhanced as it may be by our education but not inevitably lived heroically.

When I was a freshman at Notre Dame in 1951, the feast of Saint Edward on October 13 was celebrated as Founder's Day, and the university enjoyed a holiday from classes. Father Sorin's namesake was hardly well known, but Father Sorin's memory was alive. We may have lost some appreciation of our traditions at Notre Dame when we ceased the holiday and holy-day observation of Founder's Day. The requirements of calendar economy seem to have won the day. Notre Dame has chosen to let the civic holidays find their own way as well, with the exception of Martin Luther King Day, which receives a deserved affirmative action by way of academic celebration.

We need to be reminded on campus and, indeed, in our country that unless the "king" is also called to be a saint, we are in trouble one way or the other. The Kingdom of God is among us and within us, but its manifestation and triumph in the global world awaits its fulfillment in the end-time. In the meantime, put not all your trust in princes, or in kings, or in presidents, or in bishops, or in priests. Put not all your trust in accountants with certifications, nor chief executive officers with wealth, nor politicians with power, nor scholars with learning, nor even the poor and the powerless. If absolute power corrupts, so does absolute powerlessness corrupt. Imperialism and terrorism are both forms of corruption. Rather, put your trust in God and in the example of God's saints. Given that even the blessed may mean well and do harm, trust God above all, who alone can claim the divine right of king. "In God we trust" should be no empty motto on our American money.

On the day I wrote this reflection, I passed a road sign on the lawn alongside an evangelical church. "Preach the gospel always; use words if necessary."[9] In our daily life activity, we give witness to God, we confess our faith, we cry the gospel with our lives. We act out our life story in the silent motions of our days. In the spiritual life, we are all mimes. We may choose also to tell our story in words, but the story was lived first. Theology comes after faith; history comes after events; grammar comes after people speak. Jesus preached the good news in the thirty years he lived hidden and in silence in Nazareth even though we know not a word he spoke then. Blessed Brother André, C.S.C., was the porter at the door of the large school of the Brothers of Holy Cross in Montreal. He wrote no books, but his example inspired the contributions of many people, who then built a magnificent basilica to Saint Joseph. Similarly, Father Sorin and his band of brothers wrote no books, but they built with brick formed from the clay at the bottom of the lakes of Notre Dame, fired in ovens, and laid in silence, one at a time, by human hands, many thousand times over. The labor was done for Our Lady of the Lake. There lies a tale of hidden saints and unsung confessors of the faith. There lies a love story with Jesus of the Gospels, whose Father is in heaven and whose mother on earth is Mary of Nazareth, Notre Dame. "Preach the gospel always; use words if necessary." Father Edward Sorin would have understood, as surely did his namesake, Saint King Edward. Now the women and men of Notre Dame must serve in that same tradition. We are building the kingdom of God with our lives, on this campus and across the world, and we know the wilderness of historical entanglements will always challenge us as it surely did those who walked this way before us.

---

9. This saying is often attributed to Saint Francis of Assisi.

All Saints' Day: November 1

WE KNOW OF the circumstances of the deaths of many war heroes, and their graves are gratefully decorated. Not all people who served their country and gave their lives are so honored. Records become lost; bodies are never found; stories are never told. In Washington, D.C., the Tomb of the Unknown Soldier is often honored at ceremonies in Arlington National Cemetery. The unknown saints among those who gave their lives to God in hidden and unsung ways are honored in the Catholic Church with a global feast day. We shall all be called upon to lay down our lives for our heavenly country. All Saints' Day is for the forgotten, for the little people, for we who do not yet recognize the holiness of God's grace in all our lives. Think of the 10,000 students in attendance at Notre Dame, often in low profile. Consider the 5,000 employees, whose service is often unnoticed. Remember the hundreds of thousands of alums, whose lives we encounter but rarely on campus. Unknown Notre Dame saints surely abound.

Religion, when all is said and done, is about what God has done and not what we have done. Our worship of God stems from what God is doing in this our created world. We are thankful, and we praise God for such goodness. We give glory to God, who in the end remains the infinite God, who is everything, even as we are creatures somehow apart from God yet closer to God than we are to ourselves. Count the number of times, in any of our Eucharistic prayers at our liturgy, that the word "glory" appears. We come to the Eucharist to give thanks, and we come to the Eucharist to tell of the glory of God. Why is Sacred Heart Basilica gilded from floor to ceiling if not to try to reveal some inkling of the glory of God? Why such lavish and extravagant craftsmanship in every furnishing of the campus church if not to hint in our worship at God's greater glory? What we celebrate in liturgy is not what we do but what God is doing in making us children of God, unknown servants of God, and all saints.

Thanksgiving Day is a later November holiday in these United States. We are grateful for a land of milk and honey, a land of freedom and every abundance. When at times faculty or students complain about "life under the Dome," I am saddened. Of course, nothing at Notre Dame is perfect, and human beings with a share both in sinfulness and in folly are found throughout the campus. Yet pause a minute. Of course, dining-hall food is not home cooking, but a billion people elsewhere would fall on their knees for it. Notre Dame is an oasis of peace and goodness, of youthfulness and holiness, of warmth and embrace in a world grown cold in so many places. Thanksgiving Day on campus is every day, for all that we have, we have received. "What do you have that you did not receive?" (1 Cor 4:7). Hence we give thanks "always and everywhere," as the preface to our Eucharistic prayers always entreats us. And we know whom we thank and why we give thanks, and we include all those persons from whom we have received, known and unknown. We will be gathered together again in that day when all souls become all saints in the everlasting Communion of Saints in heaven. Still we remember them, and we anticipate that day when we will see them again. We pray for them, and most of all we pray with them. For those students who are away from home, immersed in a world with students from so many different backgrounds, even different countries, ethnicities, and religions, this early November reminder we call All Saints' Day seems to me a time of recognition, perhaps first that there is hidden beauty in all peoples and graced goodness in every aspect of this world, were one to have open eyes to discover all the saints.

> People are often unreasonable, illogical and self-centered.
> Forgive them anyway.
> If you are kind, people may accuse you of selfish,
>   ulterior motives.
> Be kind anyway.
> If you are successful, you will win some false friends
>   and some true enemies.
> Succeed anyway.
> If you are honest and frank, people may cheat you.
> Be honest and frank anyway.
> What you spend years building, someone could destroy
>   overnight.
> Build anyway.
> If you find serenity and happiness, people may be jealous.
> Be happy anyway.
> The good you do today, people will forget tomorrow.
> Do good anyway.
> Give the world the best you have, and it may never
>   be enough.
> Give the world the best you've got anyway.
> You see, in the final analysis, it is between you and God.
> It never was between you and them anyway.[10]

---

10. Prayer attributed to Mother Teresa of India.

Veterans Day:
November 11

ON MY WAY to celebrate mass on a Sunday at ten o'clock in the evening, I walked past the Peace Fountain (some call it the war memorial) on the west side of the library, where the old Field House of basketball fame once stood. In the dark I noticed what I thought was a statue. Closer by, I made out at each side of the fountain one of our ROTC (Reserve Officers' Training Corps) students in full uniform, silent and completely still in parade dress. From time to time they rotated in slow cadence around the fountain so that in effect, members of the air force, the army, the navy, and the marines took their turn in the complete embrace of the memorial to the veterans of our foreign wars since World War I. I was struck by their disciplined devotion to those who gave their "last full measure of devotion" in laying down their lives in the service of their country and its people.

Early this November morning, on my way to celebrate mass with a small group of regulars who come to the crypt of the Basilica before the sun is well up, I went by the Peace Fountain again. The student soldiers were still there. In shifts they had kept vigil throughout the night. How providential that on Veterans Day (November 11) we should be celebrating in the liturgy the life and death of Saint Martin of Tours. He was a Roman soldier and a saint. Legend speaks of his charity when on a cold winter night, Martin encountered a beggar. With his sword he cut in half his long cape and gave the beggar protection from the weather. Later Martin became a monk, founded monasteries in France, and was chosen bishop of Tours. One thinks of the centurion in the Gospel about whom Jesus said, "I tell you, not even in Israel have I found such faith" (Lk 7:9). And in memory of that Roman soldier, we recall his words at Communion time in our liturgy: "I am not worthy that you come under my roof. . . . But only speak the word, and let my servant be healed" (Lk 7:6–7).

In the Gospel, Jesus says if one has "faith the size of a mustard seed" (Lk 17:6), one could tell this mountain to move itself and it would throw itself into the sea (Mk 11:23). One may be disappointed in our time that the Kingdom of God on earth has not brought the peaceful end of wars and all the suffering and death they entail. But just as individual soldiers, such as Martin of Tours or Ignatius of Loyola, turned over their lives to Christ and became soldiers in the heavenly warfare to bring about the Kingdom of God, so we may yet see nations turn to the Lord above instead of to the sword. We think we now live at the end-time. We think we live in a mature and complete Christianity after some 2,000 years of progress. But we might learn a lesson from the construction of those great cathedrals of Europe during medieval times. They were not built in a day or even in a lifetime in a city scarce able to afford to build such magnificence. It took generations, several centuries in fact, to complete the best of the Gothic cathedrals. Those who laid the foundations never saw the walls, and those who built the walls never saw the stained-glass windows. In the building of the Kingdom of God, that great cathedral of living stones of we the people, we may have yet much to see. Our generation may only be laying the foundation stones. The walls and windows, the statues and the decorations, may all remain still to come. God is not finished with us yet.

In the meantime, the Gospel says, "Take care that you do not despise one of these little ones; for I tell you, in heaven their angels continually see the face of my Father in heaven" (Mt 18:10). We are not allowed to await the Kingdom while trashing those who seem but expendable pawns in a great project. Cannon fodder remains an awful term for wasting the lives of soldiers, just as abusing children or ripping off adults in a scam remains a scandal. No one is expendable. No one is less than God's beloved. And for our cavalier attitude toward life and injustice, we must give forgiveness and receive forgiveness. We are all to some degree wronged and wronging. The Gospel tells us to forgive seven times and even seven times seven (Lk 7:4). While we await the construction of the Kingdom of God on earth, there will be much forgiving to be done. But if we have faith as small as a mustard seed, then we may hope to tell our mountain of violence and injustice to cast itself into the sea of oblivion. And it shall come to pass—in due time, in God's time—the Kingdom of God promised and hoped for. And today we remember those who died in warfare wanting to give us peace.

Students who embrace nonviolent resistance to evil and students who seek to promote pacifism in one form or another argue about the rightness of the ROTC program at Notre Dame. Those student soldiers who stood watch at the Peace Fountain, where World War II, Korea, and Vietnam are named on the sides of the memorial, recognize that the issue of war and peace has many sides. At Notre Dame conscientious warriors debate conscientious objectors. I wonder whether, if we are to have warriors at all in this yet imperfect world, it would not be better to educate them well, lest the wiser people withdraw and the military be turned over to the less thoughtful. Violent but measured force to redress injustice has always been a difficult decision. Nonviolent resistance has changed the world, as in the example of Ghandi or Martin Luther King, but both of them struggled in a country where law and justice were an already established and respected order. Tyranny respects no law and order. I have often wished that Jesus had set the parable of the Good Samaritan a little earlier, so that the Good Samaritan could discover the mugging taking place. What should a "Good Samaritan" have done while the beating was taking place? How intervene? Be active or be passive? Use words or use force? And what if none of the above stopped the beating? Should one preach the cross as the Christian way to die? For oneself, choosing the cross is one thing, but choosing it for the family I am responsible for or the country whose citizens seek my protection is quite another thing. I am not sure we know what to do. We surely have divided opinion at Notre Dame. Perhaps the human Jesus would not know in the crisis moment either, though we know he would lay down his life for his people. Perhaps, for Notre Dame students, the dilemmas raised in their minds on Veterans Day give an introduction to an ambiguity in world affairs that no education, however superb, altogether overcomes.

Saint Elizabeth of Hungary: November 17

 A LOVELY STAINED-GLASS window depicting Saint Elizabeth rises tall on the east side of the nave nearest the main altar of the Basilica of the Sacred Heart on the Notre Dame campus. A Lutheran student of mine, whose name is Elizabeth, came to love that window shining in the early morning multicolored light. Our Elizabeth came from Ohio on a scholarship to Notre Dame. She was a bright student and a woman of her own. When one of my cousins, also named Elizabeth, came to look over Notre Dame as a prospective college, Elizabeth hosted her in her room in Lyons Hall. On Friday night she did not take her to a drinking party. "We don't do that," she said. "We have other ways to enjoy ourselves." They baked cookies and spent the evening in conversation. After graduation Elizabeth volunteered with the Little Brothers of the Poor in order to serve the helpless in the inner city of Chicago. One of their sayings she cherished: "Flowers before bread." First bring flowers and feed the hungry soul of the person in need, and then bread for the body. When Elizabeth married in her small town of Delphi, Ohio, I attended the wedding ceremony. Her mother became my friend, and one day she brought me wine made from tomatoes in her garden. Ohio grows a lot of tomatoes for the whole country. Elizabeth showed the goodness shaped by her mother, but I must say the daughter outdid the wine.

Elizabeth of Notre Dame was not aware of Elizabeth of Hungary at the beginning of her time at Notre Dame. I introduced her to her namesake, Elizabeth, who was held in high regard by the sisters of the Carmel of LeMans, who crafted the stained-glass windows of the Basilica. Our Elizabeth was accustomed to visit the church alone, and she told me that the saints in the windows were her grandparents. I thought of the saints also as the great-great-grandparents we never knew. Elizabeth came to love this sainted princess in central Europe in medieval times who became queen of a small kingdom. Famine was a frequent disaster in the Middle Ages. Disease or weather could wipe out a harvest, and there were no reserves. The following winter would leave little food. Elizabeth of Hungary cared for the poor and weak. From the storage of grains that her husband as king could afford, she gave away food to those in hunger. The granaries of the royal court were limited, however, and her husband soon forbade her to give away any more of their stores. She continued to be generous, and one day she met her husband on the road near the castle. He was returning from the hunt, and she was carrying loaves of bread wrapped up in her apron to distribute to the poor. It was December, as this legend of Saint Elizabeth insists, but when she opened her apron, a bouquet of roses fell to the ground: maybe legend or maybe mystery beyond our comprehension. Many are the ways the love of God can be embodied in giving of ourselves in the care of one another in this world. "Flowers before bread" comes to my mind, and Saint Elizabeth of Hungary seems to me to live again in the generosity of

Elizabeth of Notre Dame. Perhaps coincidence, more likely providence.

At the close of our lives, we will be asked only this. Did we come to love? Did we keep the one commandment, the one thing necessary, the "new commandment" Jesus gave us to "love one another as I have loved you" (Jn 15:12)? Jesus asks that we lay down our lives for others as he laid down his life on the cross for us. "No one has greater love than this, to lay down one's life for one's friends" (Jn 15:13). A daily pursuit of justice and charity with its attendant risks will be asked of us. The Center for Social Concerns[11] at the University of Notre Dame sponsors student volunteers in service projects ranging all over Michigan and Indiana and well beyond. A large percentage of our students undertake volunteer work while students at Notre Dame. Summer service projects and winter Urban Plunges sponsored by alumni clubs around the world also offer support for students concerned about the poor. The many volunteer placements that one out of ten Notre Dame students accepts after graduation testify to how concretely the pursuit of justice and the option for the poor is taken to heart. Notre Dame graduates and current students (not to mention faculty and staff at the university) have left their mark on so many endeavors for needful humanity. Consider the Shelter for the Homeless in South Bend, the Catholic Worker House in South Bend, the United Way of South Bend and beyond, the Legal Clinic in South Bend, the Holy Cross Associates, and the Alliance for Catholic Education.

---

11. The C.S.C. initials are coincidentally but appropriately identical with the C.S.C. that represents the Latin version (Congregatio a Sancta Cruce) of Congregation of [from] Holy Cross (a section within the city of Le Mans, France, where the congregation was founded).

Consider the student volunteer efforts at the Chapin Street Health Clinic; Big Brothers Big Sisters; Habitat for Humanity, which assists the owner in the building of small houses; and the countryside camp for inner-city children known as "There Are Children Here."

"Love one another as I have loved you" is a challenge and a command for each of us, whether our love is directly given to the poor or whether we serve others in need in the innumerable ways that people support people with their lives. We are all the body of Christ, whether we know it and claim it or not. "Whoever gives you a cup of cold water to drink because you bear the name of Christ will by no means lose the reward" (Mk 9:41). In the end Jesus will say to us all, whatever our belief, "Truly I tell you, just as you did it to one of the least of these who are members of my family, you did it to me" (Mt 25:40). I remain enormously proud of Notre Dame students, who give thousands of hours of devoted care and service to those in the larger South Bend community who might benefit from their enthusiasm, their heartfelt idealism, and their generosity enhanced by their education. Such volunteer service speaks well not only of them but of their family at home and their family of Notre Dame on campus.

Christ the King:
End of November

TWO FLAGS are often flown on either side of the portal entrance to the Basilica of the Sacred Heart. One enters God's house between the stars and stripes of the United States of America and the yellow and white flag of Vatican City. In the hidden recesses of our heart, the American flag is the flag of a united people of the world, and in the hidden recesses of our heart, the Vatican church comprehends all humanity loved by the one Father who created us all and the one Lord Jesus who died to save us all. However, at this moment one walks between two flags. We are all entangled with the state and with the church, with the city of man and the City of God, with the affairs of the world and the coming of the Kingdom of God. My country may seem materialistic, but many persons within it are generous and spiritual. My church may seem spiritualistic, but many persons within it are less than virtuous. Indeed, we all own to being sinful. Always we find the wheat together with the weeds (Mt 13:24–30).

The Notre Dame community must walk into its future between two flags and loyal to both, and yet a certain tension

is unavoidable. Are we Americans who happen also to be
Catholics, or are we Catholics who happen also to be
Americans? What is our true identity? What is our ultimate
loyalty? When I see the flag of my church on my right, and
the flag of my country on my left, I think I should be more
Christian than patriotic. But on the way out of church, the flag
of my people is on my right and the symbol of spiritual communion on my left. Was this tension resolved in the Holy
Roman Empire, when church and state blended as one society and one world community? Surely it was a dream never
fully realized. The union of urgent world values and important gospel values has never been integrated by political
arrangement alone. And yet politics lives to either the benefit
or the harm of our spiritual lives.

I believe our students vote for the first time in their college years. Some students may have voted at home, and some
may not go to the polls at Notre Dame. Nevertheless, Notre
Dame students will have begun to align themselves with political life. Residence halls elect their officers, and the student senate
is made up of elected officers of the student body. The debates
about war and peace, about wealth and poverty, about individual freedom and regulation for the common good, grow louder
in late-night dorm bull sessions and deepen in considered
reflection in the classroom. Whether students pull a lever or
speak their minds out loud, they have voted already in their
hearts, and it will not be long before they vote in force. Their
first educated and independently considered stand on many
contemporary issues is formed while they are university students. They know in their bones that the time will not be long
before they must take up leadership burdens in the world.

In the Gospel parable, the owner of the field has sown
wheat and seen that it was good. In the night an enemy has

come and sown weeds in the good earth. As the green blade ripens, the weeds appear as well. The farm workers would pull up the weeds, but the owner cautions against such clean-cut separation of the good from the bad. The wheat and weeds are entangled at the root. One cannot eradicate the one without hurting the other. Rather, says the owner of the field, let us be patient with the fragility of emerging life. We will wait till the harvest, and then we will separate the grain from the chaff, the wheat from the weeds, the good from the bad, the light from the dark. As the Gospel parable suggests, we also live in this world entangled between wheat and weeds, between what we would harvest and what we would discard, between what yields the bread of life and what saps our lands of energy. The good and the bad are to grow, we are told, side by side until the end, whether that be in the consummation of my life in death or in the fulfillment of the whole world at the last, in Christ's final coming. Only then will we be able to disentangle our joys and our sorrows, our graces and our sins, our blessings and our tragedies—all of our disparate flags. Christ the King, who is fully man and fully God, affirms both the kingdom of this earth and the Kingdom of God, until the end-time, when the harvest is achieved and the chaff is set aside, whether it be of our world or of our church.

Winter

Saint Nicholas

Immaculate Conception

Our Lady of Guadalupe

Information Overload

Campus Christmas

Silent Night

The Unexpected

Church Unity Octave

Saint Agnes

Martin Luther King Day and
Roe v. Wade Anniversary

Saint Thomas Aquinas

Saint Blaise

Vocation Sunday

Saint Nicholas: December 6

WHEN THE FIRST snow falls, the tradition on campus has been to greet the winter wonderland with an outdoor romp that quickly becomes a campuswide snowball fight. The university is changed into an amusement park, and the students relive their childhood delight in snow games. Schoolwork is put on hold. Snowflakes appear wonderful. Angel wings on the earth become possible, and if one can surprise someone with a shower of snow, so much more the mischievous exuberance. Fresh snow falling makes the world clean and innocent. Walking alone in drifting snow with silent footfalls and muffled sound all around can seem a moment out of time and into a world of miracles. Perhaps we never outgrow altogether our childhood, and with the first snowfall, the students reclaim their world of an earlier joyful surprise unearned. "'Twas the night before Christmas, when all through the house not a creature was stirring, not even a mouse . . . in hopes that St. Nicholas soon would be there."[1] The story of the three daughters of a nobleman whose fortunes languished remains one of the Saint Nicholas stories that wrings the human heart. No doubt we are intended to imagine three nubile maidens, attractive to the eye and noble in soul, ready and willing to give themselves to a husband and family. Because of the impoverished condition of their father, they are trapped at home with no hope of a dowry, without which no one of their nobility will court them. A young woman was born to be presented in all her loveliness. She must be the bride all bedecked in her jewels. The three maidens in the Saint Nicholas story, however, have no such gemstones. The adornment of only their own bodies and souls presents them as valuable and beautiful. In the eyes of the world around them, they are poor. It would not seem fair that women should be so limited by the demands of the men they would love and for whom they themselves in body and soul would be gift enough even without a penny to their names. Into this ancient dark story of discouragement and of lost hope for a married life and children, Bishop Saint Nicholas comes to the rescue. In the dark of night, Nicholas throws a bag of gold sufficient for a dowry into the bedroom window of the unwed maidens. For three nights he comes and throws one bag of gold in the window. As one may suspect, by the last night the father is on the watch to see who might be the savior of his house and the honor of his three daughters.

"They have no dowry," says Saint Nicholas, speaking for holy mother church. "They have no wine," says the mother of

---

1. Perhaps the most popular ballad of all time, Clement Clarke Moore's "A Visit from St. Nicholas" was written originally for his children. A friend of the family brought the poem to a newspaper, and its subsequent popularity knew no bounds.

Jesus (Jn 2:3). Let us imagine Jesus at the wedding feast in Cana when the wine runs out and the festivities are jeopardized. The bride and groom are poor; they will be embarrassed. They wanted to say that their love was priceless, and they held each other beyond cost. The lavish feast was the proof of this great love and its tangible public manifestation. At the last, Jesus provides the best wine and in quantity beyond measure. So the grace of God is ever a gift in the night, a treasure placed in our lap all unexpected, a gratuitous generosity, a graceful winter snowfall from heaven when the night is cold and dark. What a surprise, what a miracle, what a wish upon a star, and all somehow come true! God promises and it shall come to pass within God's people. A life of love is the life of the Church, and it shall be given to all of us to love. Hence the love of a man and a woman is celebrated in the Church as a sacrament of Jesus Christ, a matrimonial sacrament that confers the grace of God because the human love of this world is in Jesus married to the divine love that enfolds us each and all in God's embrace for all eternity.

I doubt our students romping in the season's first snowfall and occasionally putting a snowball through a dorm window have such thought of Saint Nicholas and the meaning of the Christmas season. But then, joy is a hint of the coming of God, and you can see delight in the faces of the young, who know deep down they too are loved. It is Christmas time.

Immaculate Conception: December 8

THE PATRONAL feast day of the Catholic Church in the United States of America celebrates the Immaculate Conception of the Blessed Virgin Mary. She is the woman who triumphs over Satan, who triumphed as serpent tempter over Eve, mother of the living. Her statue on the Dome displays her foot upon the serpent of our sinful shame. Her gaze goes out to the heavens of God, and the evil snake is trampled down. Mary is the new Eve, the new creation, the woman blessed among all women, the mother of Jesus the Christ, the mother of the Church, and the woman "clothed with the sun, with moon under her feet, and on her head a crown of twelve stars" (Rv 12:1). She is surely the First Lady of the University of Notre Dame.

When I returned to Notre Dame in 1953 after my novitiate year in Jordan, Minnesota, it was late August. During work period in the seminary, a number of us were sent to assist Father Edward O'Connor, C.S.C., in the university library, which is today Bond Hall, the home of the School of Architecture at Notre Dame. He was compiling an enormous bibliography of books and articles treating the Immaculate Conception of Mary in honor of the centennial of the proclamation of the dogma in 1854. Mary was conceived without sin. Mary was preserved from the effects of original sin from the first moment of her existence as a human being in her mother's womb.[2] I was awed by Mary's favor before God and also awed by Father O'Connor's energy, devotion, and zeal. Here was a scholar who loved the Virgin Mary and who knew how to unlock the secrets of what seemed to this young undergraduate a most arcane and intricate library of hidden resources. In 1950 this century of Mary had been rounded out with the proclamation of the dogma of the Assumption of Mary into heaven, body and soul. The Vatican Council was but a decade away. It was an exciting time in the Church.

Not everyone believes in the doctrine of "original sin," nor does everyone understand the Immaculate Conception of Mary. My students often think that the immaculate conception refers to the virginal conception of Jesus. They are not used to thinking about the origin of Mary or the origin of sin. Perhaps one could begin to understand sin's dominion by looking into purse or pocket and examining the fistful of keys we carry around with us. Why keys? One might just as well peruse the front page of the daily newspapers. How pitiful the nature of human beings if the crimes of rape, pillage, and plunder, the stories of war, torture, and treachery, to say nothing of the chronic abuse of children and of mother earth proved to be the true nature of humanity. If what we do says what we are, are we not much to be despised? What but a monstrous nature would generate monstrous crime? What if, however, all these abominations are not our human nature as created but the result of its wounded condition? Suppose our darkened mind and weakened will were

---

2. John the Baptist was thought to be delivered from original sin while yet in the womb, when his mother, Elizabeth, greeted Mary, who came to visit her with the yet unborn Jesus.

never intended from the beginning. Suppose we could hope that our wounded nature might be restored to health. Original sin is not a pessimistic statement about humanity. Original sin reminds us that human beings act sinfully because they have been wounded by sin. Given the human condition, we are sinning in part because we have been sinned against. We carry into the world the scars of human history all the way back to our origins and the beginning of sin, sin that seeded sin and sin that brought such a sinful harvest forward to this day. Sin, however, is not our true nature but its distortion. And from that distortion this one young woman, "our tainted nature's solitary boast,"[3] destined to be the Mother of God, was freed by a special grace of God in anticipation of her part in the overthrow of sin in this world through the birth, death, and resurrection of Jesus Christ. The dream of a new world from sea to shining sea in this our land, and the dream of a great Catholic university pursuing truth, goodness, and beauty in the heartland, dovetails well with belief in the immaculate conception of the Lady on the Golden Dome, Notre Dame.

I know the Golden Dome still overshadows our campus. Under Our Lady's protection, Notre Dame still lives. Visitors wonder who it is upon the top of the Dome. Some of the wild guesses are hilarious. Only Magoo could see Knute Rockne on the Dome. All of us on campus know better. When I look on the statue atop the Dome, I am reminded that neither by gender nor by racial background was this Jewish woman powerful or held in high esteem. When Notre Dame welcomes students from around the world, men and women from all cultures, whether rich or poor, the university honors the Mother of God, whose name it bears. She is the mother of the Word of God made flesh as she is the mother of our common and shared humanity taken up by God forever.

---

3. From William Wordsworth, "The Virgin."

Our Lady of Guadalupe: December 12

 IN THE BASILICA at Notre Dame, two chapels tell a story, one devoted to the old world of Europe and the other to the new world of America. The chapel in the northwest corner of the church, at the entrance to the Lady Chapel, tells the story of the Battle of Lepanto, a sea engagement between Islamic naval power and a coalition of European states. It was fought off the coast of the Slavic Balkan peninsula, where Muslim and Christian populations live to this day at cross purposes. Over centuries the Islamic world had moved across northern Africa, into Spain, and across southeastern Europe as far as the approaches to the Austrian-Hungarian empire. Had Lepanto been a disaster for the European navies, the history of Christianity and Islam might have taken a very different turn. European Christians under threat thought that the turning point was at Lepanto and that the victory was due to the public praying of the rosary. Our Lady of Victory was declared after the victory at Lepanto. In Our Lady's university in the wilderness of Indiana, that moment of peril and salvation would be remembered. Not very long ago, the poignant Ivan Mestrovic sculpture of the prodigal son being embraced by his father was moved to the Lepanto side chapel. Given the conflict growing between Christianity and Islam in our day, or between the "West" and the Arab Muslim world, the story of the two sons of a father of prodigal love, who loves them both even though neither of them understands that they are the beloved, seems appropriate. Such a father's love is never lost even if we misbehave, nor is his love won because we behave well. Such a father's love is gratuitous and unconditional, forgiving and merciful. The prodigal father is opposed to whatever in his sons seems self-destructive, not because his love is thereby wasted upon them, but because their lives thereby languish in conflict and unhappiness.

Adjacent to the Lepanto side chapel is a chapel to Our Lady of Guadalupe. A large picture of the cloth image of the Lady from heaven, who appeared to Juan Diego in Mexico at the time of the conquistadors, is displayed. The indigenous people of Central America lost the armed conflict, but they won the heart of the Blessed Mother, who appeared to Juan Diego and left her image on his cloak. Her facial features are native to the people of that region; she is one of them, and they belong to her. Our Lady of Guadalupe has given the people of Latin America to this day a proud heritage and a claim to be the beloved people of God, sons and daughters of Mary, brothers and sisters of Jesus. They were, of course, always the beloved of God as much as anyone else on the face of the earth, whatever their power, wealth, or status, but they were not told so. In this revelation of the Mother of God, however, they now could claim their graced inheritance. The recent canonization of Juan Diego by Pope John Paul II is the culmination of an irrepressible devotion to Our Lady of Guadalupe. That Notre Dame should dedicate a side chapel to her is a tribute to the growing number of Hispanic students in our midst and the widespread love of Our Lady of Guadalupe on the part of all Christians of all the Americas, north and south.

The students at Notre Dame make their first friendships here. Of course they made friends at home and in high school, but these friendships were in part an outgrowth of a home life. One could always fall back on the support of one's whole family. Alone at Notre Dame, perhaps accustomed to his or her own room at home, a student is assigned a room-mate who may be of another ethnicity, religion, or nation. Suddenly in a very small room there is another person day and night who is at first a stranger. Alone at Notre Dame, the first-year student in a residence hall of 200 unknown students may feel a bit like the indigenous Juan Diego surrounded by an alien invasion. Hispanic and gringo, Yankee and southerner, black and white, rich and poor—Notre Dame gathers them together on one campus. When Lou Holtz was asked whether there was prejudice on his football team, he quipped, "Which way?" Tolerance and respect must be learned and earned in life experience. We believe in the dignity of every human being, and the people on the Notre Dame campus strive for respectful companionship.

One of the great blessings of Notre Dame is the hearty and comprehensive residential life on the campus. Because "dormmates" live in a dedicated community, they come read-ily to cherish one another. For the first time in one's life, when one had no friend at hand, one made a friend altogether on one's own by being a friend. That first friend when one desperately needs a friend remains a unique friend. Over the years, such college-year friendships blossom. Reunions at friends' weddings, at weddings of their children, at crises of illness and accident, and during vacation interludes but fructify the friendship that blossomed early on at Notre Dame. Roommates often become lifetime friends. One can always make new friends, but as one discovers over the years, one cannot make new old friends. I like to think the Lady who long ago knew Juan Diego's deepest yearnings also knows today the desire of young students to make a loving friend and to be a loving friend, because all that heartfelt friendship flows from the love of God made man and born of the Virgin Mary.

Information Overload:
Mid-December

I LIVE AND WORK on a university campus. Long corridors in multiple buildings are traveled every day in the comings and goings that comprise the multiple tasks of academic life. Walking around is pleasant activity. One encounters colleagues and students, and there is time for a few words if desired or needed. The healthy energy of young people in their noisy rush to and fro and their effervescent vitality acts as a daily tonic. There was a time when the university did not sponsor many events beyond scheduled classes and traditional sporting events. There were a few movies, guest lectures, exhibitions, and special educational or recreational events that called for some publicity. No one would have dared, however, to mount a sign, a flyer, or a poster on the painted walls of the shabby corridors. The paint was in bad shape as it was, and taping to the corridor walls was verboten. So was cutting across the grass. But times have changed. When paths are worn across the lawns, the cement truck is not far behind. And I do not mean to carp. It makes sense to lay out the sidewalks in response to the normal traffic pattern of the pedestrians these walks are designed to serve. And perhaps it makes sense to use the corridors as bulletin boards. Sense or nonsense, we have crossed the Rubicon. Signs, we got 'em—everywhere. At first just a few signs on the pristine virginal walls seemed outrageous and surely called attention to themselves and the event, meeting, club, lecture, movie, bus trip, theater tryout, liturgical extra, whatever. More signs, advertisements, flyers, and posters appeared on the walls, then on all the walls of all the corridors, then on the doors and windows of the passages that were well traveled by all. Soon we were boasting of the excitement of the campus. We were a vibrant community with jive and jazz going on all the time. We were and we are exciting as a place to be with a cornucopia of wonderful learning opportunities of every kind one can imagine. A Catholic Disneyland the Notre Dame campus may be, a small city, circus, or museum—the intellectual stimulation is mesmerizing, and even sometimes paralyzing.

At the moment our walls are so crowded with advertisements of every color, shape, size, and texture that there is no more room. Wanting to call more attention to my event than to your event has been a challenge. Some flyers are mounted in multiples of ten or more in a row so that you cannot miss them. Others are placed at the turn of the stairwell, at eye level on doors, anywhere and everywhere you might not expect but surely cannot avoid. And in the end we have come to gridlock. The walls are now wallpapered from top to bottom and from east to west, north to south. There is hardly room for a new scrap of anything, and the ironic and hilarious outcome is this: No one notices anything, for one is paralyzed like a bumpkin on the big-city streets, a nonshopper in the supermarket aisles, a kid in the candy store, someone like me in a Barnes and Noble megabookstore. Where does one look, where does one begin, what is more important, what suits me, how do I know, will I remember, do I care, and what am I missing in this blooming confusion that is so beautiful, so touching, so young and idealistic, so erotic and spiritual? We want it all. We surely love the true, the good, the beautiful. Here is the smorgasbord of life, and our unfocused eyes are even bigger than our stomachs. Do we ever want it all! We want a big place in the sun. We want to be noticed. We want to lead. We want to have something to give and to offer to others. We just want, and we want a lot.

Our contemporary culture seems to me to be drowning in excess information about everything that means almost nothing in the end. The amount of data from newspapers, television, e-mail, bulletin boards, paper mail, voice mail, advertisements, posters, billboards, pagers, and cell phones dwarfs the gossip of the beauty salon and the barroom of an older day. As Wordsworth wrote long ago, "The world is too much with us." Undergraduate students need someone who talks to them with an awareness that they may be caught in a web of confusion. Each course can seem to be self-contained. Courses can seem to be, and may actually be, opposing, even if not contradictory. One argument cancels out another, and one perspective is countered quickly by an alternative. In the end a university education may seem all too Socratic. What we come to know is that we do not know very much. Humble learning remains a virtue, of course, but what one hopes for is also some integration of the educational endeavor. We would give students a home in the intellectual world. We would give students an education designed by an architect. We would give them a balanced meal and not a smorgasbord. The role of philosophy, theology, and spirituality has never been more needed in higher education. We do not want to graduate confused students, skeptical students, or disenchanted students. We want humble students, but students who have an idea about how all learning fits together even if the details escape us. Though it may be slow, the pursuit of truth remains possible. We promise our students that they can live in confidence and in hope.

I often describe college education as the renovation of one's childhood world. Most students come from homes where they were taught true and false, right and wrong, proper and improper. They were explained these verities in terms suitable to growing children. In college they may be told that their justifications are somewhat oversimplified. Their intellectual world needs to be renovated. They need plumbing and wiring brought up to code. The roof will have to be repaired and even some of the foundation stones reset. In the meantime they will have to live in the backyard in a tent. In the end, their newly renovated home will be much the better, and nothing of value will be lost, but rather it will be protected with explanations suitable to their adult education. College education at Notre Dame remains a blessing. Fifty years ago at Notre Dame, the focus was less panoramic, but the viewpoint may have been sharper in its philosophy and theology. We want and need both—breadth and depth—the world and the faith. When the whole picture makes sense and we know where the endless details belong, Catholic education is indeed a great blessing.

Campus Christmas: Advent

EVERY YEAR right after Thanksgiving, as if the campus could bloom flowers in late autumn, university workers versed in complicated wiring hang Christmas lights to decorate the prominent evergreen trees one cannot pass without noticing. As I rock on the porch of Sorin Hall, I am watching a lovely tall evergreen tree between the Basilica and the Dome building. It is covered with lights of every color right to its top, and the tree twinkles as it sways in a breeze in the early dawn darkness of a wet, cold, and lonely Saturday. All the world seems abed, but there is the tree, awake and aflame with light.

As I watched alone this lone tree in blazing color, I became fascinated with the twinkling of its lights. Perhaps all trees are the "burning bushes" of the Moses story (Ex 3:1–6), and perhaps all moments are afire with God's light in them if we have eyes to see them and to recognize their kaleidoscopic beauty. So it seemed to me this morning. The lights were on every bush and tree, and I but lacked eyes to see what God wrought there. Lights we do not see are sparkling all around us, for God is everywhere, and his revelation our surprise.

Such hopefulness may to some seem like singing in the rain or whistling in the dark. To me it is the coloring of the blackness that threatens our human hearts. What are we doing here as specks on this burned-out cinder in a vast and cold, apparently impersonal universe? Why anything? In this ever-green tree that shines with colored lights in the middle of a rainy, cold winter dawn, I see the rainbow that Noah saw after the flood receded. I see the dawn of God's people alight with grace and destined for eternal life. I see the coming of the day of God's infinite light that lends color to all our existence and beyond the farthest star. Christmas lights are hopeful lights that counter the despair that deepens the night.

> How precious is your steadfast love, O God!
> All people may take refuge in the shadow of your wings.
> They feast on the abundance of your house, and you
>   give them drink from the river of your delights.
> For with you is the fountain of life: in your light we
>   see light.
>
> (Ps 36:7–9)

The Notre Dame campus gathers more and more colored lights as Advent wears on. Residence hall Christmas displays vary in quality, but no dorm is ever dark. Depending on the imagination and generosity of students busy with many things at the end of the academic semester, Christmas decorations appear out of nowhere in the middle of the night. We are told that Advent is a time of patient and prayerful waiting for the coming of Christmas celebration. However, one begins to hear "Joy to the World" even before Thanksgiving Day. After Christmas, one hardly hears a Christmas carol again. The commercialization of Christmas plays into the academic schedule all too well. As children most of us could hardly wait for our presents on Christmas, and many of us were known to anticipate with a peek at what was to come. Perhaps we have not altogether left that Christmas of our past memory. Christmas on the campus has to come before the students leave the campus for Christmas at home. In some ways, Advent season has become not so much a time of restrained preparation as a pep rally for the big day. I am not sure that development is all bad. The last Sunday mass of Advent season on campus becomes in each residence hall a poignant event. The university is a campus home, and soon campus will be empty. Our students go to their parental home. Christmas must be anticipated with those with whom they have lived Advent.

One of these years Notre Dame will win again a national football championship. It is bound to happen. Providence demands it, we do believe at Notre Dame. Some people thought it would happen in the very first coaching year of Tyrone Willingham. Students say they fear it might happen after they graduate from Notre Dame. How unfair! And what about tickets for the alums? This celebratory anticipation and this sense of providential inevitability suggest what the early Christians felt with regard to the Second Coming of Jesus Christ. They knew that it would happen one of these years, and they thought the great day of victory and celebration was coming sooner rather than later. Like the students, they did not think it fair that some of their loved ones had graduated by their deaths into the next world. Were they going to miss it all? What about their promised place at the Second Coming?

Christians talk of the Kingdom of God being present now and to come. Jesus is present now. "And remember, I am with you always, to the end of the age" (Mt 28:20). And Jesus is to come "on the clouds of heaven with power and great glory" (Mt 24:30). We await the Second Coming while we enjoy his first coming at Bethlehem, a presence extended through the coming of the Holy Spirit at Pentecost and in our own baptismal share as Christians. Even now our bodies are "temples of the Holy Spirit" (1 Cor 6:19). We celebrate the real presence of Jesus here and now in the Eucharistic bread of every Sunday. Christ is "the same yesterday and today and forever" (Heb 13:8). And yet we live by faith. Heaven is now and yet to come. "For now we see in a mirror, dimly, but then we will see face to face. Now I know only in part; then I will know fully, even as I have been fully known" (1 Cor 13:12). I like to give my students this comparison: Let us suppose you win the state lottery. You are no longer poor; you are rich. You have the winning ticket in your hand, but you as yet have not a nickel in your pocket. Similarly, we hold the treasure of eternal life with God in our hands by faith, though we have not yet the joys of heaven on this earth. We have heaven now because with God's presence and love dwelling within us, we have the essence of heaven. It is Christmas always.

Silent Night:
December 25

LONG AGO a man and a woman journeyed to the sleepy town of Bethlehem. A child was born. Angels in the sky sang, "Glory to God and peace on earth to everyone of good will." There were shepherds in the field abiding their flocks by night, and they came to see the newborn child. I am not sure why the Christian tradition imagines Mary gave birth at midnight. I suppose we celebrate midnight mass because we want to begin the new day as soon as possible so that the celebration of the day the world stood still might be as long as possible. I am not sure why we believe it was a "silent night" when the Creator of the universe was born a little baby that "made a woman cry."

If truth be told, the power of God is not in the explosion of creation or the music of the spheres. The absolute awesome infinity of the eternal God, the almighty and uncreated existence from whom and in whom and for whom all else exists, dwells in silence. Not silence that is the absence of sound and the emptiness of air, but silence that is the consummate fullness of all that is. And God spoke the Word of creation that would make a world from nothing. And God spoke out of the silence his own Word, made our mortal flesh, to share our destiny of noise in the collisions of our conflicting ways of this world. The most loved song of Christmastide and perhaps of all time is the German folk tune composed as almost an afterthought. "Silent Night" brings tears to our eyes.

> Silent night, holy night!
> All is calm, all is bright
> 'Round yon Virgin Mother and Child.
> Holy Infant, so tender and mild,
> Sleep in heavenly peace!
>
> . . . .
> Silent night, holy night!
> Son of God, love's pure light,
>
> . . . .
> Jesus, Lord, at thy birth.

Silence and night, and who would have thought that the fullness of time and the fullness of eternity were hidden in the deep silence in the middle of the night.

I believe that our students make a second first Communion on Christmas day of their first year at Notre Dame. Of course, most of the students who are Christian have known a first Holy Communion long before they came to the university. But that moment in their life was within the embrace and example of a family and a church. Now they come back into their family and their hometown church as adults who have left home and come back on their own. Their brief education already has changed their perspectives. They see their home, their church, and their religion with the eyes of the campus family who questioned them for deeper understandings and the books that challenged them. Now Communion is much more their decision, made more on their own two feet, a merger not only of the present and the past but of the present and their future with God. The first Christmas back home is a "first" Holy Communion in many ways.

The twelve days of Christmas have become famous through the popular song that concludes each verse with "a partridge in a pear tree." A sumptuous feast for the imagination is provided by those extravagant lyrics, and pundits have even calculated the fortune it would take to assemble this mini Noah's Ark. The story of the three kings—or three astrologers, or three magi, or three wise men—continues to fascinate us. We are not sure there were three of them, but because there were three gifts, tradition provides three gift givers. As commentary on Matthew's Gospel unfolded, they were even given names—Caspar, Melchior, and Balthazar. Artists painted them and traditionally thought one of them more dark skinned. Gian Carlo Menotti's beloved opera *Amahl and the Night Visitors* has even given them a script and beautiful deep voices. George Macdonald, in his poem "The Holy Thing," wrote of them: "They were all looking for a king / To slay their foes, and lift them high; Thou cam'st, a little baby thing / That made a woman cry." (As one commentator noted, three wise women "would have asked directions, arrived on time, helped deliver the baby, cleaned the stable, made a casserole, brought practical gifts and there would be Peace on Earth.")[4]

Wise men still seek the King of Kings, born humbly in Bethlehem. And wise women seek him as well. One hopes with all one's soul that university education and the pursuit of wisdom lead our students to Christ and never away from the unquestioned faith of childhood. Learning and the love of God should be a duet in the soul that ever sings of the infinite

4. Attributed to Tom Morrow, staff writer for the *North County Times*, dated December 16, 2000.

mystery of God. The wise men recognized the star that led to Jesus; even the ox and ass knew where they were fed in the manger. Do we recognize Jesus in the breaking of the bread on our altar and the daily bread on our table at home? Do we recognize our students at the university, who remain the sole reason for the whole structure and all its personnel, as they truly are—the beloved of God the Father, the body of Christ, and temples of the Holy Spirit? In this earthly life we are at times misled and confused. We mistake what we love and whom we love. We do not recognize the love divine in our human loves, the Lord Jesus in this child Jesus, the love of God in the vicissitudes and delays, obstacles, and seeming tragedies of our love life in this broken world. Yet beyond our entanglements, the compassionate mercy of God ever awaits us.

The Last Judgment will be not a day of wrath and reckoning, as we might conjecture in our vengeful human imagination. Judgment Day will be an epiphany day. We will see the ways of God revealed. We will know how suffering was necessary to allow love to deepen. We will see how all the pieces of the jigsaw puzzle of this world's history do fit together to make the loveliest white rose, a vision of the Communion of Saints gathered together in Dante's visionary paradise beyond the stars. We shall see how every event or person that enters our life belongs to it and fits in the puzzle somewhere. We may be working with a corner of blue pieces and wonder what we will do with these red pieces. But they belong in the "Godscape" somehow and somewhere. We must wait for the revelation of love and for the epiphany of God. And when we see a gap in the pieces of our puzzled life, we must believe that the missing piece will be given us. We will find the child lying in the manger that all along we have been seeking—the missing piece fulfilling the picture of God's love in this world.

The Unexpected:
Early January

ON A MIDWINTER Sunday morning when I was walking around Saint Mary's Lake, I saw a tall dead tree whose naked branches high above the water were crowded with large birds sitting in contemplation of the sparkling lake surface in the light of the rising sun. Probably they were hunting for a meal to appear that they would pounce upon, or perhaps they were observing a fitting Sabbath rest. At first I thought they must be hawks or possibly even turkey vultures, but surely they were predator birds perched so high and mighty, surveying the world below at their mercy. When I came quite close to the tree, there sat the birds, but I recognized them for what they were. These were wood ducks, preening their feathers and quite comfortable high in a tree. Queer ducks, no doubt, for we think ducks live in the water or along its banks. Not so. Wood ducks nest in the trees, and they clearly enjoy their perch.

We can all learn something from the unexpected. We learn from the world around us as a child in fascination examines everything from the bug in the grass to the cracks in the sidewalk. Alas, our spiritual sense of wonder, along with our

bodily muscles, tends to atrophy as we age. We no longer read
books to learn something new. We read to confirm what we
have already concluded and now defend against change. We
no longer look up words in the dictionary. We assume our
vocabulary is sufficient and the author has chosen to obfuscate
his or her writings with words seldom used and unnecessarily
employed. In short, rather than learn from ever new and ever
deeper experience, we impose our previously learned experience upon the present moment. We look for what we expect.
And we do not expect to see ducks in the trees. We conclude
they are not normal. Indeed, they are queer ducks. They are
not normal if one means by normal the average waterfowl
by statistical count. And yet they are wonderful and beautiful.
The world is a better place because wood ducks create a variety and a beauty of form and behavior all their own. To see
them with wonder-filled eyes is to see them as new and nothing to fear.

The campus of Notre Dame does not escape the tensions
of the society at large or of the world in regard to the presence
of homosexual men and women. Many in our society find gay
human beings different from the norm. We judge them abnor-
mal in a sense that carries many definitions, from rare and val-
ued to perverted and unwanted. And we know so little about
gay people, unless by the mercy of God someone we know and
love tells us of their life as a gay person. In truth, gay people
grace the world with an array of human talents. Star athletes
and star artists, star theologians and star statesmen—gay and les-
bian people are everywhere if we would care to look without
prejudice at the world as fashioned by the Creator and not the
world as we expect to find it. We all need to hear what Jesus
heard from the heavens at his baptism: "You are my beloved in
whom I am well pleased." The question is never so much who

I am as *whose I am*. We all belong to God our Father as beloved sons and daughters. In a prayer to the Blessed Virgin Mary, given out at Sunday masses on campus in order to promote the unity of the Notre Dame family, we pray:

> Please bid our Father to open our minds; that each of us will come to know the unity of which God is source and destiny. Ask your Son to infuse our hearts with courage, to act against ignorance, intolerance, and injustice. Call upon the Holy Spirit that we might celebrate the diversity in our midst. Move us to welcome and value lesbian and gay members of this family. Inspire us to include all creation into the circle of God's love and our community. By our Baptism and new life in Christ, direct our journey back to the Father's Son and Creator, and draw us together as companions on the way.

Church Unity Octave: Mid-January

THE TWO WORLD wars are ancient history for our students. They were not even alive when Christian nations of Europe tore each other apart in appalling violence twice in the twentieth century. The European Union stems not so much from a theory of federalism as the better government as from the recognition that there must never be a World War III. The world has become a global village, and the "internetting" of communication, commerce, travel, and culture beckons us forward to one world order. While weapons of mass destruction may be at their worst, the hope of global world peace may be at its best. National wars may be things of the past in the not-too-distant future. Our world has become thoroughly inter-national. And our students know that future already in their bones. Their comfort with the computer age and their eagerness to study abroad in the many international programs offered by Notre Dame do not surprise me. Many are the places Notre Dame sends its students in its own programs: Angers, France; Dublin, Ireland; Rome, Italy; Nagoya, Japan; Monterrey and Puebla, Mexico; Toledo, Spain; Perth, Australia; and Washington, D.C.

They already think nothing of travel that yesteryear would have seemed extraordinary. They already wish to be of service in countries whose language and culture they are able to appropriate as a matter of course. There is a global awareness in our students that comes with their age, and Notre Dame encourages them to think big.

Nothing is worse than civil war. When Abraham Lincoln quoted the Gospel passage that argues, "No house divided against itself can stand," he affirmed what at heart we all know. When we kill our brother or our sister, we kill ourselves. The Cain and Abel story in Genesis is the first murder the Hebrew Scriptures record and raises the perennial issue: We remain our brother's and sister's keeper, and our lives remain always interdependent and entwined. Hegel called history "a butcher's block," for the taking of human life greatly saddens the human story. Aware that all sentient life lives off some other life that must perish, the poet called nature "red in tooth and claw."[5] Tribal warfare, plunder, piracy, national wars, and empire all have this in common: Human beings prey on each other, and, alas, it is no surprise. That the Church of Jesus Christ would suffer division and religious wars, however, was not expected. Jesus died to bring everyone together in peace as children of God. We are all one body, one spirit, in Christ. The descent of the Holy Spirit at Pentecost enabled Peter to speak the one language of love for brother and sister that everyone from the nations of the world gathered in Jerusalem for the feast could understand. Pentecost was the Tower of Babel[6] story of confusion of tongues and human purpose leading to the division of rivalry and inevitable warfare, but now told in reverse and

---

5. Alfred, Lord Tennyson.

6. Genesis 11:1–9.

undone. The Holy Spirit was the spirit of unity and peace. Thus the great scandal of Christendom is our division, and the great sadness of all the world religions is our suspicion that we have not done God's work always and everywhere to bring us together as one people, the people of God, who no longer engage in internecine war and who no longer build a house divided and unable to stand.

Church Unity Octave is observed every mid-January with a week of prayer for the unification of Christendom. The World Council of Churches initiated this endeavor, and world meetings of all Christian groups from time to time have attempted to bring about this widespread desire for unity in Christendom.[7] So many of the ancient theological disagreements between Christian churches have been resolved in recent times by collegial dialogues and conferences. Because the majority of Christians now dwell in the Southern Hemisphere, the older issues of theological dispute and political division of Europe may seem less relevant. Perhaps the day of unification of Western Christianity has begun to dawn. Global Christianity surely encourages this unification.

World religions and their common search for God pose yet another challenge for Church unity. If Christianity is the one true Church, what should be said for Judaism, for Hinduism, for Islam, for Buddhism? The Holy Spirit remains the same

---

7. Roman Catholics were invited to participate in the meeting of the World Council of Churches, but out of concern that the numbers would be skewed by such participation, Catholic observers were sent instead in order to represent the Roman Catholic point of view. Eastern Orthodox Christianity is seen more as a schism or separation within the one Church than as a division of the one Church of Christ.

one spirit given to all human beings, and that Holy Spirit is a Spirit of Unity. All truth comes from the Holy Spirit, and no truth is foreign to the Holy Spirit. I would like to think if any thoughtful religion were to purify its doctrines of distortion, the truth that would remain would be accepted eagerly by all Christians, who would but offer in Jesus Christ a unique fulfillment desired but unfound in a world unaware of the mystery of the Incarnation. Christianity also needs to purify its doctrines of distortion and the representation of its doctrines in so many inadequate ways in the faith education and way of life of many of its people. That purification of any and all religions in order to state clearly and accurately the truth of God discovered or revealed remains a complicated endeavor. A Catholic university provides the place where the church can do its thinking and try out innovation yet remain faithful to Catholic tradition.

Wisdom in these matters comes only with age. Every generation begins anew, and distortions once eliminated emerge again. Yet we are people of hope who believe that the Holy Spirit and the grace of God are given to every human being. The resourcefulness of God to bring humanity together remains our hope. To speak with our students of religious unity, of welcome and respect for other religions, does not surprise them. International Festival Week showcases the diversity of the student body: cricket, hurling, Gaelic football, Czech-Slovak Food for Thought Dinner, French Coffee House, Brazilian Samba, and much more in the way of literature, displays, fashion shows, food, and dance. They already know in their bones that isolation and separatism are dead. Only a world unified and a church unified will well survive tomorrow.

Saint Agnes:
January 21

WHEN I WAS fifteen years old, I knew, instinctively perhaps or even mystically, what my inner self deeply desired. I was in love with Saint Agnes, virgin and martyr.[8] Adolescents all have crushes. I imagined her as a beautiful young Roman woman my age who wanted to love God above all else and who refused to marry the suitor pressed upon her. And she would die to preserve the exclusive love of God that enveloped her soul and her whole life. She was beautiful in body and even more beautiful in soul, and I loved her. Later in my adolescence, I loved Princess Elizabeth, crowned queen so young, and Elizabeth Taylor, of *Cleopatra* fame. I was young, and I was born and raised in Elizabeth, New Jersey. All

---

8. "**Agnes** (died circa A.D. 304) Of a wealthy Roman family and noted for her beauty, she early resolved to live a life of purity, consecrating her virginity to God. She was denounced as a Christian to the governor during Diocletian's persecution by unsuccessful suitors and though only thirteen refused to be intimidated by the governor's display of instruments of torture. Infuriated, he sent her to a house of prostitution in Rome, where she successfully retained her purity by her saintly bearing, and in one instance by a miracle. When returned to the governor, he ordered her beheaded, which was done. (Some

the Elizabeths have since faded in my fascination, but Saint Agnes has grown into even more of a mystery, and her hold on my imagination and heart has riven my soul. The only prayer I ever composed in my life was conceived in my adolescence at Saint Benedict's Preparatory School in Newark, New Jersey. I say it often to this day. "Saint Agnes, virgin martyr, who loved her purity above all else, help me to preserve mine; who suffered terrible tortures for the love of God, increase my love; who suffered martyrdom, strengthen me in time of persecution." Dante Alighieri fell in love with love when he saw Beatrice, a young noblewoman of Florence whom he would encounter on the way to Sunday church. In a moment he had seen a vision of love itself in the loveliness of this particular woman, whom he desired far more than he could explain. Sensuality and spirituality are such an implicate mystery. Human love and divine love seem to crisscross in these adolescent crushes or mystical graces. What should one call these soulful epiphanies? I hear the cynic saying they are but hormonal exuberance, and I hear myself saying that we discount the most exquisite and delicate graces of our lives out of our ignorance and fear of God's overwhelming love for us.

I recall vividly the time when I was a freshman at Notre Dame some fifty-plus years ago and heard the hesitant early efforts of a Notre Dame orchestra performing in the huge Navy Drill Hall that stood where the Hesburgh Library now

---

authorities believe she was stabbed in the throat.) Although much of her story is unreliable, there is no doubt that Agnes suffered martyrdom and was buried on the Via Nomentana, where a cemetery is named after her. Over the centuries she has become the great Christian symbol of virginal innocence, usually represented in art by a lamb [*Agnus* in Latin means lamb]." John J. Delaney, *Dictionary of Saints*, abridged ed. (New York: Doubleday, 1983), 26.

stands. I heard a solo violin, and I watched the delicate fingers and arm of the woman who played a melody that moved my inner being. How romantic, one might say, and perhaps so. I own to weeping at the death of Princess Diana, and I would sign on with Edgar Allan Poe that nothing is so sad in this life as the early and tragic death of a beautiful woman.

One of the students I have come to know in my recent years at Notre Dame has greatly charmed and inspired this campus. A folk singer and guitarist in love with God, she enkindles an enthusiasm rarely seen and almost never shared so widely. In concerts and in dorm liturgies she has moved the hearts of Notre Dame students. Danielle Rose tells of her first song and the lyrics she made up as an adolescent in her initial discovery of God's love for her. I made a point of memorizing those lyrics when I first heard them, for I was touched deeply. Later, in one of her concerts, she turned the same lyrics into a love song for a boyfriend, and I was reminded that our human quest for love both heavenly and earthly is not yet at its end.

> Do you love me? Say you do!
> Do you really want me too?
> Say you'll think of me twelve hours out of seven.
> Do you need me? Say you do!
> Say you'd cry if I were blue.
> Say you'd rather be with me than another.

As I am writing this reflection about a Notre Dame woman student with a gift of song and a heartfelt public devotion to God and remembering my own devotion to Saint Agnes, virgin martyr, the Catholic Church is in the middle of a sexual abuse scandal rampant in the United States. Millions in money and ruin in morale are all detailed in the news media. It is not only that abuse of children is so damaging and heartrending, or that gay sex can be so promiscuous, or that bishops can engage in dubious damage control that does not protect the victim, the priest, or the Church. What is eroded the most is the love affair that is at the heart of the incarnational religion that is Christianity. Our purposes become so distorted. We were to cherish the flesh, not disrespect it; we were to guard the sheep, not fleece them. Not only how bad the scandal, but how sad. Saint Agnes, virgin martyr, pray for us.

Martin Luther King Day and *Roe v. Wade* Anniversary: Latter Days of January

 IT MAY SEEM strange to yoke together in one reflection the anniversary celebration of Martin Luther King and the anniversary of the Supreme Court decision asserting a woman's constitutional right to choose an abortion.[9] Both these days are observed with intensity and public demonstration. There are gatherings and speeches. At the end of the day, we are more aware how far we yet remain from the Kingdom of God. Blacks are not yet fully free. Women and children are not yet fully free. Memories of slavery and its attempted justification, even using Christian scriptures and religion, yet linger. Memories of spousal abuse and child abuse remind women that they have reason yet to be wary. Respect for life continues to challenge our moral response and our perseverance in a struggle that remains tenacious. Paul's

---

9. Martin Luther King Day is celebrated on the third Monday in January. The anniversary of *Roe v. Wade* is January 22.

claim remains our hope: "There is no longer Jew or Greek, there is no longer slave or free, there is no longer male and female; for all of you are one in Christ Jesus" (Gal 3:28). Were Paul alive today, he might add: "no longer Muslim or Christian, born or unborn, young or old, sick or well, rich or poor." Therefore respect life. Respect the human person. Think of the reality of our lives. Only human beings live forever. I think of those simple words that Rodney King said after his beating at the hands of police (and I am mindful that his own record of behavior was not always civil): "Can't we just get along?" That's not very far from "Little children, let us love, not in word or speech, but in truth and action" (1 Jn 3:18).

On the Notre Dame campus, Martin Luther King Day is celebrated with pride and with campuswide planning, speeches and choirs, and special events and remembrances. A distinguished speaker brings to mind the timeless advice that "eternal vigilance is the price of freedom." Blacks are not very numerous on campus, and if one subtracted the athletes, they would be markedly less so. Most African American students are not Catholic, and the culture of Notre Dame for racial as well as religious reasons remains less than a perfect fit. Prejudice on campus in word or deed, at least openly, is not notable. That blacks band together in their social life on campus, in their groupings, and in their leisure activity may be inevitable, and perhaps whites do much the same. Perhaps suspicion or just "like likes like" fuels our reluctance or inability to overcome our differences. The history of slavery in this free country of ours has left a scar. I often think that the violence of the spectacle lynchings and abuse of black men, women, and children might have been resisted with a wave of terrorism in this country. That Martin Luther King led the march to freedom with nonviolence has been a blessing that deserves a national holiday for its annual celebration.

No one I have ever known has ever said abortion was a positive experience. Some people I know tolerate abortion. About the procedure, everyone from the mother to the medical personnel is ambivalent at best and lifeless at worst. Notre Dame students by the busload every year attend the rally in Washington, D.C., on the anniversary of *Roe v. Wade*. Vigils at the South Bend abortion clinics are supported by the "right to life" chapter of students on campus. I am always touched by their fervor and their indignation. The Women's Care Centers, which provide support and long-term assistance to any unwed mother, were initiated by Janet Smith, who taught in the Great Books Program at Notre Dame, where I myself teach. Perhaps living with abortion these many years has made some of us callous to its devastations. Perhaps we are paralyzed with the skepticism that the tide cannot be turned. Perhaps we are perplexed with a biological world of conception hardly understood in its complexity and where nature itself wastes so many conceptions that do not implant. We all yearn for a solution that will unite us in respect for unborn life and no longer divide us so bitterly. The problem, however, remains so much more than one issue. Preaching on abortion in developed countries seems like preaching on stealing in undeveloped countries. So much about us needs change.

Education designed to respect everyone remains a crucial task in our universities as well as in our homes. If there is any hope for humanity on planet Earth, it resides in coming generations of human beings who have been treated with respect, given every opportunity to mature, and educated and inspired well in mind, heart, and soul. The University of Notre Dame has no better claim on our loyalty, support, and generosity than its mission to educate both the mind in the best learning and the heart in the pursuit of justice for everyone, regardless of age, ethnicity, gender, or whatever.

Saint Thomas Aquinas: January 28

 WHEN I WAS a seminarian at the old Moreau Seminary, which still stands along the northwest shore of Saint Joseph's Lake, we were all required to choose philosophy as our major sequence in our undergraduate education at Notre Dame. Philosophy would prepare us for the study of theology in preparation for ordination to the priesthood. Not just any philosophy would serve well; it was the comprehensive medieval synthesis of faith and reason elaborated by Saint Thomas Aquinas that yielded the best instrument for a faith seeking understanding. I am grateful to this day.

Precisely because Thomas covered every pertinent question and every objection thought of in his time, he offered a student of his writings a panoramic map of an intellectual world. We students did not understand as much as we should have, perhaps, but we had our bearings. We knew where north was, and all the other points of the compass could be deduced. My students today speak of their disappointment that the pluralistic intellectual world of today, for all its wonderful variety and insight, has deprived them of a reliable framework.

When Father Hesburgh became president of Notre Dame in 1952, he appointed Father Charles Sheedy, C.S.C., dean of the College of Arts and Letters. Many of us in Holy Cross highly regarded him for his wisdom, his wit, his magnanimous humanity. He taught us that the essence of community life is simply "showing up," that is, attending all the family events with regularity regardless of one's mood. A student is reported to have called him to complain of not receiving an A in one of his courses and requested to come talk to him about grades. As the story goes, Father Sheedy replied that he would give the A, no questions asked, if the student promised not to come and talk to him about grades. Father Sheedy read voraciously, and he devoured the latest and most difficult books reviewed in the *New York Times*. The rest of us leaned on his comprehensive and integral learning. We were kept abreast by his commentaries. We knew that those authors who attacked faith or disparaged reason had been read by him, considered, and placed within the critique of a Catholic tradition that could once more absorb the many objections, especially those come round again from long ago. In short, Father Sheedy was like an ocean reef, and when the storm waves of contradiction threatened the frail boat of our faith, we small craft took refuge in the harbor protected by his capacious mind and heart. I like to think that the University of Notre Dame provides such harbor to all its students today as well.

In the philosophical world that Thomas Aquinas knew so comprehensively, one hears of a division of philosophers into lumpers and splitters, that is, those who find unity in multiplicity and those who insist that the particulars of the real world are incommensurable. Accordingly, the lumpers take after Plato, and the splitters take after Aristotle. The lumpers might more easily include poetry and wisdom and the splitters, language analysis and empirical science. Christian faith recognizes that in God, all being is somehow One within the infinity of God, and in creation, all beings are somehow Many within a finite world. Only God could have it both ways, infinite unity of divinity and incalculable multiplicity of creation.

We human beings would have our cake and eat it too. We would hold on to both faith and reason, both Catholic and university, both eternity and time, both divine worship and human dignity, both grace and freedom. We believe that the world is meaningful and human destiny hopeful. Sin is the only non-sense. Although we want to take the road to happiness, we insist sinfully and foolishly on taking a road that does not go there. As the practical farmer said to the city slicker, "You can't get there from here." The Catholic marriage of philosophy and theology celebrated most elaborately by Thomas Aquinas would argue that our world, even in its misery, is by no means the "tale told by an idiot, full of sound and fury."[10] Rather our world—with an ear tuned to the Word of God—hears the music of the spheres and the song of the angels. Ultimately our claim is that the Word of God did in truth become flesh. God became man. The human condition is not absurd. It is blessed. Light, not might, rules the world, even if we await the dawn of the everlasting light.

If human beings are capable of seeing God, if our destiny is eternal joy as the friend of God in the Communion of Saints, human beings must be capable of knowing truth. Although we should own our debacles and our abominations, our Calibans and our Gollums, we need not despair. We are "such stuff as dreams are made of."[11] We are the stuff of heavenly glory. The Church does not canonize the thought of any

---

10. Shakespeare, *Macbeth*.
11. Shakespeare, *The Tempest*.

particular theologian. The Church does canonize the sanctity of his or her life and devotion to God. We do not give medals for thought alone.[12] Thomas Aquinas defended the human mind in its capacity to know God, and he loved God in the mind's capacity to know God. With all his metaphysical learning, Thomas Aquinas speaks of the Eucharist with quite poignant devotion. His Latin hymns, such as the "Pange Lingua" and "O Salutaris Hostia," are sung to this day. At Notre Dame, adoration of the Blessed Sacrament is presented in the Basilica on First Fridays, and all-night adoration once a week in Fisher Hall began in response to student initiatives.

When all is said and done, our students still dearly need and want a centering of their education. The faculty members share this need and desire in their own lives. We differ at times on the means to that end. On the feast day of Saint Thomas Aquinas, I am always reminded that we all search for wisdom whatever our way, and the wisdom of the past perdures, even if its expression must be earned, honed, and rethought in every generation.

---

12. The Laetare Medal is given annually by the University of Notre Dame to a person distinguished for public life as a Catholic.

Saint Blaise:
February 3

OF THE MANY rituals connected with the saints and the many intercessions of patron saints for every imaginable sickness and need, only the blessing of Saint Blaise for illness of the throat seems to have perdured through the centuries. One still marvels at the assembly of the faithful accustomed to daily mass who remain at the end of the Eucharist to walk again to the altar to receive a blessing from the priest, who places two crossed candles before the throat of each recipient of the blessing of Blaise: "By the intercession of Saint Blaise, may the Lord deliver you from every illness of the throat and every other evil." The scene is a remarkable witness to a bygone era of devotion to the saints and the power of blessings from the patronal saint of a particular human need in a world that still remains in many ways a "vale of tears."

When the students of Notre Dame come back from every corner of the world after Christmas break, a grand contamination with hitherto unfought viruses is likely. The campus is afloat with pathogens once the students return with cold viruses tailored to their homeland. To top off this scene, which

I exaggerate, but only slightly, students typically come to my office with essay in hand and coughing loudly. Since they are hoarse, they move closer to me and breathe in my face so I can hear them. "Cough, cough. Professor, I am so sick; I just came by to tell you that I am too sick to attend your class and am about to check myself in at the infirmary. Cough, cough." It is at this time that I join the line of devout believers and ask for the blessing of Saint Blaise. It is not only my faith that needs the grace of God and a helping hand. I know my respiration is in dire risk.

A legend about Saint Blaise connects his healing with the preceding day in the Church calendar—Candlemas, February 2. It was on this day, as Bishop Saint Blaise was blessing candles in the cathedral, that a child began to choke. Blaise took up the blessed candles and said a prayer, and the child was cured—hence the blessing of throats with the blessed candles on the feast of Saint Blaise immediately following Candlemas day.

Not many holy days in the Church calendar are such a puzzle as "candle-mass" day. According to ancient tradition, the faithful on this day would bring a year's supply of household candles to the morning Eucharist. During the course of the mass, these candles would be blessed. The light in one's home for the coming year would thus be blessed light; indeed, it would be the light of Christ. Jesus came to birth in the stable in Bethlehem during the darkest days of the year. He came as the dawn, as the coming of the light of the world, as a light that shines in the darkness. In the Gospel passage of this day, which is also called the "purification day of Mary," she comes into the Temple in Jerusalem to perform the rite of purification as prescribed by the law. Because childbirth involved shedding blood, a woman was held in a kind of quarantine, as were others afflicted with an illness involving loss of blood.

Hence women came to the Temple some weeks after child-birth, when they would receive a ritual lifting of the quarantine. In the case of the firstborn child, the woman also offered a sacrifice to signify spiritually the handing over of the life of the newborn to God, the giver of all life. So Mary comes into the Temple with Jesus in her arms to present him to God. She offers two turtledoves in sacrifice, in the usual gesture of the poor, who could afford to sacrifice no more valuable life. A poor, humble young woman with her firstborn male child in her arms comes into the vast Temple of God in Jerusalem. She comes as a living candle holding in her arms the flame from which all light has its birth. She is the candle and he is the flame. She carries the light of the world in her arms. The Temple is then filled with the light of God, who in the beginning said, "Let there be Light" (Gn 1:3). On the anniversary of this day, the followers of Jesus and Mary centuries later bring their candles to the church of God for a blessing so that throughout the year in their homes, they may harbor the light of Christ beheld so luminously in the humanity of their children and indeed in the humanity of us all.

> O star of wonder, star of night,
> Star with royal beauty bright,
> Westward leading, still proceeding,
> Guide us to thy perfect Light.[13]

---

13. From the hymn "We Three Kings of Orient Are."

Vocation Sunday:
Early February

IN 2002 "Vocation Sunday" fell on Super Bowl Sunday. The bishop of Fort Wayne/South Bend sent a letter requesting that the homily of the day focus on vocations to the "consecrated life." The vocation office of the Congregation of Holy Cross on the campus seconded the idea with a letter of its own. The scene was set on this winter Sunday as a light snow drifted over the campus. Most of the evening masses in the student residence halls were scheduled to begin fifteen minutes after the close of the game. Super Bowl XXXVI began with an almost creedal résumé of the founding documents and traditions of our American democracy. Past presidents and distinguished surrogates seemed almost a litany of saints. Some months had passed since that unforgettable September 11 that so challenged the meaning of our lives.

At halftime the music group U2, from Ireland, sang with a vigor matched only by the crowd's enthusiastic syncopation and wild applause. I thought of the upcoming homily of our mass in Pangborn Hall and wondered if I stood a chance of generating such rapt attention and obvious delight. I know the lyrics of U2's songs, not because I can decipher the song words, but because my students gave me a CD of their music and a paper copy of their lyrics. South Bend had but recently hosted U2 in the Joyce Center to a throng of townies and students, who seemed appreciative despite the cost of their tickets. Because some of the profit and much of the message serves well the cause of justice and peace in the world, the musical talent of this group appeals to the generous souls of the young at heart. They thirst for a better world, and they would not only pray for it but play for it and pay for it.

I thought all this Super Bowl hype was secular liturgy at its magnificent best, and again I wondered how well our homegrown dorm liturgy would compare at game's end. The Super Bowl game of 2002 would have matched any of its predecessors for strategy, courage, and a suspenseful winning field goal with no time left on the clock. Somehow the patriotic theme of the entire Super Bowl liturgy, the flags, and the heightened security of our armed forces at the stadium gates all dovetailed superbly when the New England Patriots won the game, just as their forebears stood strong at the Boston Tea Party and prevailed at the end of the Revolutionary War, which the underrated colonies were never supposed to win against the British superpower of the day.

When the game was over, I walked to Pangborn Hall for my moment with a sacred liturgy, which might well prove to be anticlimactic. The chapel began to fill with students, although not as many men as usual came to this women's residence hall Sunday mass. Super Bowl parties spilled over, and perhaps the men indulge more enthusiastically in the spectacle and the libations required to endure the tension and the inevitable sorrowful outcome when only one team can win. A moderate number of the women, mostly residents, came willingly and

quietly to the simple yet elegant Pangborn chapel. The beati-
tudes were the Gospel reading. Vocation Sunday was the
theme. My homily was to be brief and to focus on the "consecrated life" of the women and men who give their lives in
the various approved congregations and orders of the Catholic
Church. There was a time not long ago when we would have
said "religious life," but I think we rightly now want to say that
everyone has a religious life, and that all confessing Christians
surely have both need and desire to enhance their religious life
given them in their baptismal faith. What I said about vocations to the publicly consecrated life followed a simple anal-
ogy. My claim insisted that at the heart of this public vocation
is a desire to find God—to know and to love and to serve
Jesus our Lord in one another. The consecrated life remains
the radical public expression of the baptismal consecration and
mission of every Christian.

If one were passionate about skiing, I think one would likely
join a ski club. In company with other passionate skiers who
wished to give their lives to this pursuit of excellence, one would
find instruction, advice, companionship, hints and secrets of
the sport, special opportunities to acquire equipment, and
access to the best-known trails. In a congregation of sisters, or
brothers, or priests in community, one does find a passion for
God that kindles the passion to make the world a better place.
Love of God truly is inseparable from love of neighbor. The consecrated life in its active congregations has spent itself in endeavors to better the education, health, and welfare of those in need,
whether at home or abroad, whether of the faith or not. The
Lord Jesus loves us all, and to love him is to love everyone.

My remarks after the Gospel concluded with a descrip-
tion of what makes any vocation a genuine vocation, whether
it be marriage, career, or church. Does this way of life give you

life and allow you to give life? There are no sad saints, even though there be suffering saints. Joy is the mark of our loving God in the ways that fit our soul. Not that there will not be dark days, and even sorrow and failure, but through even those times we know an inner joy, "and no one will take your joy from you" (Jn 16:22). At the kiss of peace in this simple liturgy, now seeming such a quiet contrast with the Super Bowl extravaganza, we the people of the Church were players on the field and not spectators in our easy chairs. I thought how wonderful and grace-filled each of these women truly was in the eyes of God and in my own, which dimly mirrored, I thought, how God saw them. I hoped one or more of these students might be called to the consecrated life as a sister or brother in Christ with a public profession of devotion.

I found myself at the closing blessing of this "Vocation Sunday" immensely grateful for my own vocation to the vowed life and priesthood, and I was truly hopeful that some of these graced young women and men would try out the "consecrated life" in the Church. After all, "You did not choose me, but I chose you" (Jn 15:16). In the end, everyone has a vocation from God to be who they were created to be and in so doing to serve God's people. Notre Dame students today have almost too many occupational choices. With their multiple talents, they could do so many things. But, most of all, they are the beloved of God, and their vocation remains to love as they are loved. May God bless them and call them forth.

Spring

Saint Valentine's Day

Sophomore Literary Festival

Junior Parents Weekend

Ash Wednesday

The Lenten Season

Spring Break Week

Saint Patrick

Stations of the Cross

Saint Joseph

The Annunciation of the Incarnation

Holy Week

Ordination Day

The Fisher Regatta

Final Exam Week

Graduation Day

Saint Valentine's Day: February 14

VALENTINE'S DAY at Notre Dame brings mixed feelings. I smile at the young men moving across campus with flowers, walking briskly and holding the red roses gingerly, as if the flowers would deliver a burn if touched. In the ripening air of springtime, Tennyson tells us, "A young man's fancy lightly turns to thoughts of love." Many of the women (and men) on campus wait for a card from a significant other. I think my mixed feelings stem from knowing that on this day some are exuberant and others disappointed, and the sadness is magnified as in an echo chamber by the joyfulness of the blessed ones running about. Perhaps only the day of "room picks" in the residence halls equals the pain of not being noticed, or included, or chosen, or in any way being special to the one to whom one so wanted to be special. Valentine's Day can be difficult. We all want to be first in somebody's heart. We know God made us special. When others neglect us, we are depressed because we know we deserve better. As Sebastian Moore says: "I exist and the world should dance." I am the beloved of God, and there is no one else quite like me. Each of us is uniquely wonderful. We want to be admired and cherished.

The poignant question raised on Valentine's Day could be raised every day: Does anyone want me?

Mid-February is the time of year when the first nesting songs of the birds in the British Isles were heard after the winter. If you listen, you will notice the birds (particularly the cardinals) at Notre Dame begin their territorial nesting songs in mid-February every year. If the birds are setting about the business of family life, should not man and woman take the hint and begin their courtship song? Written cards are more convenient than a window serenade, but the idea is the same. A little-known martyr of the early Church, Saint Valentine (whose feast day is February 14) lent his name to these rites of spring. Chaucer's poem of long ago says it all so much better:

> Now welcome, summer, with your sun and softness,
> That has this winter's weathers overshaken,
> And driven away the longest night of blackness!
> Saint Valentine, who are in lofty highness,
> For your sake sing the birds in all their smallness,
> Now welcome, summer, with your sun and softness,
> That has this winter's weathers overshaken.
> Well have they cause to often sound their gladness,
> Since each of them his mate again has taken,
> Full blissful may they sing when they awaken:
> Now welcome, summer, with your sun and softness,
> That has this winter's weathers overshaken,
> And driven away the longest night of blackness![1]

---

1. Version composed by Dolores Warwick Frese for her father, Charles Carroll Warwick. Used with permission.

Shakespeare in perhaps his last play has the lovely and innocent Miranda lay eyes on a young man, the only man beside her aged father and the uncivilized Caliban that she has ever seen in her island exile. Instantly she falls in love. When she subsequently encounters the entourage of her prince charming, she exclaims: "How beauteous mankind is! O brave new world that has such people in it!" (*The Tempest*, 5.1). Miranda proclaims an innocent love, the delight of Adam and Eve when love first bloomed in the garden. "This at last is bone of my bones, and flesh of my flesh" (Gn 2:23). The love of man and woman celebrated so exquisitely in the Song of Songs echoes that delight. "Arise, my love, my fair one, and come away; for now the winter is past, the rain is over and gone" (Sg 2:10–11). Perhaps we are all too accustomed to human beings to marvel at their intricate and delicate loveliness of body and soul. We have been numbed by the trashing of human beings in war, in ethnic cleansing, and in the slow deaths of poverty, injustice, famine, and plague. Yet not one of us could make with our hands the many-faceted eye of a common fly nor the minuscule needle of a mosquito. Ponder then what a tremendous work of creation is the human being—body, soul, mind, and heart—destined for eternal life as friend of the infinite and all-encompassing God, who created everything from minute bacteria to galaxies of giant stars.

Early in the morning of this Valentine's Day I was walking around the God-quad in front of the Main Building. The roadway has been rebuilt in the form of a heart, as the original designers had planned. The statue of the Sacred Heart stands in the center of that quadrangle. Walking around the heart-shaped driveway over and over again in the early sunshine of a February day, I seemed to walk about in the heart of God's love. Where love is, God is found; where God is, love is found.

The whole student body seemed to speak to me of that heart's desire. The yearning of us all is to find the love of God in the love affair that is our lifetime. Valentine's Day seemed no idle celebration of the human heart. Suddenly I broke my stride and turned up the direct sidewalk leading to the Dome. It occurred to me in walking the heart's path to God that the human heart was all too often broken. Jesus would have understood the love of the martyr, Valentine.

Students tell me there is not as much old-time dating at Notre Dame now that we have a coed university. Women and men join together for classes and meals. They "date" in groupings of friends, and they hang out together. Students still become engaged to marry, of course, and some are known to be casual about sex. Most students, however, are more likely to agree with a letter to the editor in the *Observer* from some time ago. The author urged a chaste friendship with the women one came to know at Notre Dame, and he was thankful so many of them had remained his friends whom he could visit over the years since graduation. He argued that friendships that become overly intimate romances and then split apart make awkward any lifelong friendship in days to come. Valentine's Day comes around every year, and those we have loved well, we love forever. To cherish the human heart as sacred remains the best Valentine.

Sophomore Literary Festival: Mid-February

AFTER WORLD WAR II both more ambition and more money colored life at Notre Dame. The desire to become a great Catholic university began to have wings. Notre Dame grew as never before under the presidency of Father Theodore Hesburgh, C.S.C. It was, however, the dean of the College of Arts and Letters who encouraged what is now called the Sophomore Literary Festival. Father Charles Sheedy, C.S.C., supported the sophomore students' initiatives to stimulate creative writing and overall appreciation of literature on campus. Money was raised from various resources in order to invite contemporary writers to read their work here and spend time with students, who would choose them, host them, introduce them, and converse with them. Over the years this week-long festival has brought to campus many authors whose names one readily recognizes. The very first festival, in 1968, made history in more ways than one. The story is detailed in the Festival Guide:

> The festival finally took shape with the impressive line-up of Wright Morris, Ralph Ellison, Granville

Hicks, William F. Buckley, Joseph Heller, Kurt Vonnegut, and Norman Mailer. The event received national attention when its group of writers and international film critics came to Notre Dame for the première of Norman Mailer's film "Beyond the Law." Turbulent political events marked the week of Mroz's festival [Mroz was the student initiator]. Tension was building over the Vietnam War and the protests. President Johnson announced his decision not to seek reelection. Martin Luther King, Jr. was assassinated. Joseph Heller was having dinner at Professor John Matthias' home when King's assassination was reported. Granville Hicks, a week-long participant in the festival, later wrote in the "Saturday Review," "I was sorry for Heller last evening, for he felt as he said, that a reading from *Catch-22* was inappropriate to the occasion, but there was nothing else he could do." Ralph Ellison noted his reactions to the event during his lecture, and Wright Morris excused himself from the closing symposium. [All] of the authors invited were activists for various causes, thus providing an appropriate commentary on the times. Despite the political events, an important week at Notre Dame had evolved.

The Sophomore Literary Festival has remained a long and strong tradition at Notre Dame. This midwinter week continues to be a wordfest for wordsmiths, including our own campus poets and writers, whose work is also read. Two of my students over the years have chaired this event—Betsy Harkins of Mississippi and Katie Ellgass of Indiana. I have attended many of these festivals, and I want to leave the reader with a flavor of what I take away—a poem here and a story there, a few notes scribbled on scrap paper in the excitement of the moment, a memory of a writer who compassionately understands the human condition, who makes me feel less alone, and who reassures me that what I have felt and dared not say or didn't know how to say does not make me a freak. Let me quote one of my favorite poems from one of these annual early February evenings. I imagine the poem might be set in our own Basilica of the Sacred Heart:

> Then, you were a hot-thinking, thin-lidded tinderbox.
> Losing your balance meant nothing at all. You would
> pour through the aisles in the highest cathedrals,
> careening deftly as patriarchs brooded.
> You made the long corridors ring, tintinnabular
> echoes exploring the pounded cold floor,
> forcing the walls to the truth of your progress:
> there was a person in this church's core.
> Past thick stained-glass colors wafted and swirling
> in pooled interludes that swung down from the rafters,
> cinnabar wounds threw light on your face, where the
> pliant young bones were dissolving in laughter.[2]

In Luke's Gospel, Jesus encounters a blind beggar beside the road through Jericho before it begins its serpentine path upward to Jerusalem (Lk 18:35–42). Jesus stops and faces him. "What do you want of me," Jesus asks him. A simple question, it would seem, but one we all have a difficult time to answer. What do I really want from life, in my life, for my life? So

---

2. "Running in Church," in *Eve: Poems by Annie Finch* (Ashland, Oreg.: Story Line Press, 1997), 2. Used with permission.

many things I wanted in the past I no longer want, and disappointment makes us all wary of pinpointing what we want with too much hope. The blind man begs only one thing: "I want to see." And I want to echo his cry of the heart. I too want to see. I want to see God. The artists of our world write with eyes eager to see and hearts passionately seeking insight. We are all in some way Tiresias, the blind prophet, who speaks a deeper truth than eye can see. We are Oedipus, the despised sinner who blinds himself and in the darkness learns the wisdom of the inner light. We are all blind beggars on the roadside in Jericho as Jesus goes by in his ascent to Jerusalem and his destiny with the cross of Calvary hill. In the beatific vision of God in eternity, we shall see light itself and the beauty that the painters sought with figure, that the poets sought with words, that all of us seek with the loves of our lives as we become artists of the spiritual life and storytellers of God's grace experienced and made tangible. The Sophomore Literary Festival renews my hope to see, for I want so very much to see everything.

Junior Parents Weekend: Late February

JUNIOR PARENTS WEEKEND at Notre Dame has become a heart-touching visit of mothers and fathers, who are hosted by their children. What is said and done on this weekend leaves a memory treasured by everyone involved on campus. Typically the weather in late February presents dark, cold winter. Some years these parents show their love in just fighting the elements and arriving in South Bend at all. One hears stories of parents stranded in the Chicago airport who rented cars and drove together to Notre Dame despite the snowstorm. The heartfelt invitation and the response, notwithstanding an inconvenient journey, reveal how often the medium is the message. Parents love their children, and on this weekend their children tell them of their love in hospitality given and perhaps also in words spoken.

I have always thought the junior year the best of the four years of college. In the first year of studies (called freshman year before coeducation), the students are not yet altogether here. Part of each of them is homesick. Sophomores have read all of Plato but do not know they do not know. In their salad days, they are crisp but quite green. Seniors are already part gone, for their heart has already begun to imagine the future and to prepare to say good-bye. But the juniors are here body and soul, and they are in the main mature in mind and in heart. They seem to me at their best as college students. It was in my own junior year at Notre Dame that I experienced the only one certifiable and dramatic conversion of my life. Prior to that year I studied the teachers and not the courses. I did what I had to do to stay out of trouble and remain in favor, but I did not do what I wanted to do. I was involved in studies like someone reluctantly on a diet or irritably repressed by a public code of moral behavior. I was dutiful in study but not in love with truth. I started to read Tolstoy's *War and Peace* and set it down a few days later as too much effort and a bore. Suddenly, by whatever grace and minor miracle, I changed inside my head and heart. I wanted to learn. I wanted to know the truth about everything. I wanted to know that I knew. I wanted to read every book in the library. I took up again *War and Peace* and thought I had died and gone to heaven. I almost remember the day and the hour of that conversion, which became a lifetime erotic yearning to be one with the Truth in its infinite and ineffable implications. I could not tell you the cause other than a belief that God wanted me to pursue God in the pursuit of this newfound love affair with Wisdom. All this change happened in my junior year at Notre Dame. And I have known and taught junior-class students who are so alive with the yearning to know, so capable of generous heart combined with ample knowledge. They remain grateful and thoughtful, ready in every way to host on campus the mother and father who gave them life, who taught them to tie their shoes, and who gave them human language and family love as the wealth of kings and queens—and paid their tuition and more at Notre Dame. Junior Parents Weekend is simply wonderful.

Perhaps the flavor of this Notre Dame family weekend might best be appreciated in the prepared remarks of one of our students in the Great Books Program:

Moms and Dads, you give us much more than we realize sometimes, and much more than we're willing to admit most of the time. You have given us the gift of life and love, a home and all that is necessary to live, the values, the system of beliefs, and the sense of right and wrong that makes us the people we are. You give us your advice and understanding when we need it most, and even when we're too afraid to ask. You have incredible patience, which must seem hard to maintain at times, and you have the knack of accepting the good as well as the bad news with a sympathetic and forgiving ear. You give us a sense of responsibility, which makes us work hard and remain determined to succeed, and you give us support and encouragement we need when our goals seem out of reach. You give us the time and space in which to grow, and very generously, you have given us this education, which at times must seem the greatest gift of all. In other words, you have given us your very selves from the moment we were yours, and for this we will forever love and thank you. Moms and Dads, above all of these things is the fact that you have given us freedom, and you knew when it was time to let us go. Two and a half years ago, we came to this university very different people than we are today. We have made new friends, learned somewhat to live on our own, and we have started the process of living away from you. We've entered into a new family now, but the home that we return to each Christmas will always be "home," and this family will provide us with many memories after we leave this place. Professors, you challenge us to question things for ourselves and then find the answers. You open new doors in front of us and close old ones behind, and you bring us a better understanding of wisdom, truth, goodness, beauty, and justice. You also are patient and compassionate, and there are times when we are utterly relieved to discover that you—like our parents at home—are human too. You give us the love of learning by your enthusiasm, and you have a way of making things enjoyable even on the coldest and darkest winter days. We thank you for your professionalism within the classroom and your friendship and guidance that make our education much more than knowledge of the Great Books. By no means are the things I have mentioned here a complete list of everything that we have to be thankful for. We are as well indebted to our friends and classmates for the laughter, the insights, and the friendships which we enjoy in each of our classes. We learn from each other, and our closeness comes from the knowledge that we are a part of a very unique and wonderful group of people. Parents, as you travel home this weekend, please know that we, your sons and daughters, are in very good hands in this Program—this special family that we call PLS [Program of Liberal Studies]—and also know that we love and thank you very much.[3]

---

3. Text delivered at a PLS luncheon on Junior Parents Weekend, February 2, 1987.

Ash Wednesday:
Early March

CHURCHES ARE crowded on Ash Wednesday. No one is obliged to attend on this weekday, and no special encouragement has been given over the years to the faithful. Perhaps we know in our hearts we are sinners, and we know we need help. Whatever the reason, Ash Wednesday has become a popular ritual, and the reception of ashes, a sign of human and Christian solidarity. We want to own our membership in a church of sinners who are mortal. In the expulsion of Adam and Eve from the Garden of Eden, the Lord God rebukes Adam: "By the sweat of your face you shall eat bread until you return to the ground, for out of it you were taken; you are dust, and to dust you shall return" (Gn 3:19). In our church liturgy we echo these last words: "Remember you are dust, and to dust you shall return." That's us, and the smudge on the forehead is worn in public almost as a badge of honor. We are dust of the earth, the humble dirt out of which God created Adam before he blew the breath of life into Adam's nostrils (Gn 2:7). We weep and we bleed; we laugh and we give birth; we know and we love in a human body made of some earth and warm water in a very fragile envelope. We all die. It behooves us to be humble because of our humble origins. The word "humble" is derived from the Latin word *humus*, which means exactly what one might buy as potting soil. On Ash Wednesday we acknowledge that we are earthen ashes, our body next to nothing.

Planet Earth is a tiny, burnt-out cinder in an enormous cosmos, and each of us but a speck of dust upon the surface of that cinder. One of the beloved professors at Notre Dame used to ask students where the nearest desert was. Arizona or Montana might have been suggested, but his answer was the desert some few inches below the topsoil. We are fragile life on a thin crust of a cinder that is itself a speck in an incomprehensibly vast universe of stars and debris. And yet we are more than dirt. Every molecule of our body and of planet Earth was once vibrant in a star. We are made truly of stardust. As awesome in astronomical distance as a voyage beyond the cosmos must seem, we come honestly by our desire to travel beyond the stars. We know in our bones planet Earth is not our final home. We are cosmic orphans, trying to find a way back to where we belong in God's creative love.

If one looks in the side chapel to the east of the Lady Chapel at the rear of the Basilica at Notre Dame, one can inspect a large collection of relics of the saints, encased in jeweled and enameled reliquaries. Bone relics were first-class relics, and they were held to be as precious as a piece of moon rock—and for a similar reason. With much effort mankind made its way to the moon and brought back samples beyond this earth and its life. The tiny fragment of bone of the body of a saint was thought to be already a piece of heaven and eternity held in hand on earth. In the resurrection of the body at the end of the world, those very bones would rise to live forever. This body was guaranteed a place in heaven, and so with a bone relic of a saint, one already had a sacred piece of the world to come beyond moon, sun, stars, and the limits of this cosmic universe. In his or her body, this saint would see the face of God and live. And so might we hope, even of Ash Wednesday.

Muriel Spark's thoughtful novel *Memento Mori* takes place in a nursing home amid the various selfish and graceful responses which the elderly make to one another and to the reality of their suffering and their pending death. "Memento mori" (remember you are going to die) is the message that the protagonist in the novel receives in frequent anonymous phone calls. Our mortality is the one thing we must not forget, lest we forget who we are. "Ring around the rosy, pocketful of posies. Achou! Achou! ["ashes ashes" in a somewhat distorted but understandable construal of a fatal coughing infection] we all fall down" is a children's jingle for play, but its origin may stem from the dreadful period of the black death in Europe during much of the fourteenth century, when half or more of village populations died suddenly and painfully of a devastating plague. "Memento mori." Remember you are going to die. Amnesia is the greatest risk of the spiritual life. We forget where we came from and where we are going. We lose track of our journey through life with death. We hardly know our true name. And so we pray on Ash Wednesday not to forget who we are. Not any of us shall get out of this predicament alive. "Remember, man, you are dust and unto dust you shall return." For our students at Notre Dame, Ash Wednesday may be a first heartfelt public confession of their mortality, on their own, away from home, parental support, and routine observances.

The Lenten Season

THE SEASON of Lent prepares the Church for the celebration of Easter. The season of Lent was designed particularly as a preparation of the catechumens who were to be baptized at the Easter vigil. The season of Lent was also a time of prayer, fasting, and penance for the faithful in the pews who wished to repair their spiritual lives and prepare themselves to enter into the paschal mystery of Holy Week with a full heart and a generous resolution to walk the walk of the gospel and not just talk the talk. We were all to confirm our baptism and renew our acceptance of the goodness of God's unconditional love in the death and resurrection of Our Lord Jesus Christ.

Those of us with pre–Vatican II memories recall the everyday Eucharistic fast from food and even water from midnight until morning Communion time. Many of us can also remember our Lenten penances as children. We were too young for adult fasting. Instead, we gave up candy, and in the days of twenty-five-cent allowances, we saved our pitiful small change in a cardboard slotted box designed to hold our petty sacrifices. It was a beginning, and for a youngster a good bit. Self-denial made for a habit of life. The Lenten tradition still lives, and most people I know give up something for Lent or add some good work in preparation for Easter.

Whenever I watch the evening news, I become convinced our nation has become a culture of drugs. Indigestion, headache, backache all warrant drugs—and no doubt innocent, legal, and therapeutic drugs—but we push drugs. On every college campus, the drug of choice comes not from the pharmacy but from the liquor store. Alcohol seems prescribed on the campuses of our country, and in excess it afflicts the bodies and the souls of our young students. They are initiated into drinking by weekend parties, which for all too many students become a habitual way of life. *In vino veritas* (the truth comes out in wine) does not seem the primary motive. Abusive alcoholic consumption more likely comes as an escape from the tension, effort, burden, competition, and confusion of demanding life choices. Young college-age men and women continue to have a problem with overconsumption of alcohol, and Notre Dame has tried with many initiatives to make self-responsibility part of a college education. Were a student to seek to observe the ancient Lenten fasting and penance, I can think of nothing better than to give up alcohol and put the purchase money in a piggy bank to be broken open on Easter morning as a donation for those who do not have even fresh water to drink.

Fasting as a discipline of body and soul even to this day has merit. Our spiritual life is all too flabby. As a spiritual jog, as a purification, as an effort, surely fasting from some food and some drink is good exercise for spiritual couch potatoes. But of the Lenten fasting and discipline yet more can be said. Let us claim fasting and self-denial are an attempt to enter into solidarity with the hungry and poor of the world, who are fasting out of necessity and not out of choice. Let us, by our self-denial and "fasting" from whatever substance or deleterious habit, in our spiritual life willingly and deliberately enter into a humble solidarity with an afflicted humanity. Let us say and mean that "there but for the grace of God go I." A friend of mine told me of visiting an addict in prison, where in the cold-turkey therapy of a cold jail cell he found his friend in the agonies of withdrawal from substance abuse. When my friend finished his visit, he went outside to light up a cigarette, but he could not do so, overwhelmed as he was with the memory of the pain he knew forced "fasting" was inflicting on his friend. We cannot sit down in good conscience to a banquet of food and drink when the hungry of this world stand outside our dining-room door, if we open our eyes to see them.

There is one last commentary on Lenten "fasting" or "spiritual effort" that I would offer. The lives of Christian monastics were given over to the pursuit of the love of God and of a close spiritual union with God in Jesus Christ. These men and women experienced both periods of great spiritual feasting and periods of spiritual famine. Desolation of soul, dryness in prayer, and loss of fervor were terrible trials in the monastic life. In times like this, they could recall that when they felt deeply in love with God, food did not seem important. Lovers gladly skip a meal to be with the beloved and to prolong their spiritual conversation. Who needs food when one is at the banquet table of love? In a humble and poignant attempt to reverse their malaise, the monks concluded that maybe if they went without food and its importance as they did at the height of their fervor, just maybe their love for God in its intensity would be renewed. They fasted to rekindle a love affair with God. Our struggle to know and to love God needs a Lenten season as well. Overeating or overdrinking can foster a sour love affair with material goods because our soul remains so lonely and so hopeless without the God we unknowingly love. The penances of Lent are in the end the searching of our heart's desire for the joy of the presence of the beloved that can never be taken away, even by the deprivation of death. "Remember you are going to die." Ash Wednesday.

Spring Break Week: Mid-March

SPRING BREAK comes always in the knick of time. Perhaps because they know that a vacation week is coming, both students and faculty plan their second-semester energy to last only till that harbor is reached. No doubt we all have the winter blahs by the middle of March, and cabin fever rages, especially in the young. Many students in college work harder than may appear on the surface. Competition both academic and social is keen. Tension and exhaustion, misery and depression are not reserved for those making a living. Those living where the living is supposed to be easy know better.

The break does not come in the middle of the semester. Midterm exams are given during the seventh week. Spring break begins the week after. When they return, students are often surprised at how fast the six remaining weeks fly by. Papers are due, and final exams are looming. The weather is improving, and spring fever is rising. As with many a horse race, the winner is determined at the last turn and in the stretch run to the finishing line. In midwinter, going anywhere and getting away from here does some good, no matter the itinerary.

Some students go home, some go far away to Cancun or Paris, and a few students stay on campus. Students from a foreign country are more likely to be stranded. Most of our students head for the beaches of Florida, Texas, and Mexico, where being stranded is fun in the sun. This professor stays home and corrects term papers, scheduled adroitly to allow for days of leisurely reading, both to give the students a more thorough critique and also to keep my own mind from the frazzle of too many essays per day. To all their own. But no doubt the beach trips are the spring breaks that students tend to dream of.

They head to both of the Florida coasts. They head to Padre Island in Texas. They move to Mexico. They travel in caravans, friends with friends. They triple up to lower motel bills. Coming back with a tan is required proof of the trip and established bragging rights. Wild stories may or may not be true. A good many less-than-balanced meals are washed down with more than enough beer. It's spring break in college. We have been fantasizing about it ever since such stories were narrated to us. Spring break can be a wonderful time with friends in a leisure that campus never quite provides. Spring break may be a week to remember or a week to forget. Some overdo the sudden relaxation of all restraints in a foreign and flirtatiously romantic land. Some imitate others and come back home to a recognition that they were doing what others were doing and not what they wanted to be doing. The herd mentality may capture a student especially in the first March on campus.

I think spring break is a last fling of childhood exuberance carried out with adult resources. This springtime bash challenges the deeper values of students who want something else and something more. One learns of a considerable number of students who spend their spring vacation helping people out in Appalachia or assisting the poor in Mexico. Simple home-building projects are well received because after a week of a combined effort, one can see that the group who came to help made a difference. One group of students went to Cuba this past year to witness the struggle of the Church in that country. Some students travel to spiritual retreats, such as the Trappist monastery of Thomas Merton fame in Gethsemani, Kentucky. Some students stay in their residence halls and work on their study projects. They cluster together out of loneliness in a dormitory more than half empty. Pizza parties and time for conversation can lead one to discover the goodness of one's friends and the convenience of the campus, both perhaps much taken for granted before spring break. Local students spend time at home, and many of them take the stranded students to their homes for a day or two. Foreign students, especially, find themselves adopted by generous students who live in the vicinity.

Given the spring break, one wonders why the Easter holiday finds students again heading away from campus, despite a vacation week not so long ago and despite the end of the semester only a few weeks away. Perhaps South Bend weather inevitably drives students to warmer and sunnier climes. As the story goes, when Father Sorin arrived at Notre Dame du Lac in December of 1842, the Brothers of Holy Cross who accompanied him pleaded with him to settle the university farther south. One imagines that Florida would not have been out of the question. Father Sorin is reported to have reassured the brethren that they would indeed move farther south just as soon as the weather improved in South Bend. And the rest is history.

Saint Patrick: March 17

THE "FIGHTING" of the Irish was not originally done on the gridiron of the University of Notre Dame. That "fight song" came later. The Irish fought to be American in a Waspish country that all too often thought uneducated Catholics need not apply. The Irish fought for the democratic dream of freedom of religion and equality of education and opportunity. They came to America to fight for the life they were denied in Ireland. They came because of widespread famine at home.

The students of Notre Dame are mostly Catholic, and the Irish are more than mostly Catholic. When the Ku Klux Klan in the early 1900s moved on South Bend in hostile ways, they were met with resistance by students of this Catholic university. One likes to think today that the "fight" has been won, and that we play now only a ritual game with a football on autumn Saturday afternoons. The Irish Leprechaun icon with fists upraised has been seen by most people as cute and by some as inappropriately bellicose. And yet we know that eternal vigilance is the price of freedom, and perhaps all freedom-loving people must perpetually struggle ever to be mindful of their past and watchful over the present in hopeful providence for the future. Saint Patrick's Day at its best reminds us all, whether Irish by birth or Irish by adoption, that we need to prize our spiritual and our political freedoms.

Patrick is the patron saint of Ireland. One needs to understand the origin and the role of patron saints. In the early Church, the Christians were for the most part among the poor and the powerless. In the Roman Empire, families of wealth, status, or influence owned access of some kind to the court of the emperor. Those befriended by the mighty and the powerful referred to their benefactors as patrons (from the Latin word *pater*, or father in the wide sense of provider and protector). Patronage was the order of the day and the way the Roman world went round. High-powered lobbying in our own day offers a close parallel. One needed to know someone to have something done. One needed access to the throne and insider suasion. To gain the ear of the emperor, one needed a patron who had the ear of the emperor and stood close to the throne of absolute power.

Christianity brought about a thoroughly democratic revolution in the system of patronage. Now every child was to be baptized with the name of a saint known to be at the court of the Most High in heaven. That saint would be the child's patron, his or her own patron saint, whose intercession with the Lord God could be called upon day or night. Shrines to the saints were Christian churches open to everyone, rich or poor, high born or low born. Everyone was equal in prayer before the patron saint enshrined. Everyone was granted an audience. The rich might bring gift offerings, but the gospel theology proclaimed that God's graces could not be bought, but only sought and freely given.

Countries as well as individuals were given patron saints so that the national interest and the populace of the country at large might be represented before the throne of God. Saint

Patrick spoke for the Irish and interceded for them according to their prayers. The Irish knew all about second-class-citizen treatment, whether at home in Ireland or as immigrants on foreign shores. They honor to this day Saint Patrick because they remember, some more than others, the way of the world compared to the way of the Kingdom of God, where in truth the poor and the powerless make equal claim to God's largesse.

Saint Patrick's Day celebrations are legendary. From the parades of pride in major cities to the pub parties with a pint of bitters and then some, the Irish know how to party. The "Fighting Irish" of Notre Dame are no exception, and the campus parties are occasions for some happy memories and sometimes woeful regrets. Celebrations of legendary fame can entice students to excesses. One of the learning experiences of college years demands recognition that choices have consequences. If one becomes intoxicated, one is still responsible for damage done to life, limb, and property, even if the next morning one cannot remember what it was all about. Sometimes I think the university is delighted that Saint Patrick's Day usually falls during spring break. The troubles of the few who cannot contain themselves do not trouble the campus. And yet, trouble is a teaching moment. I know that alums come back to the university to see their rectors more than their teachers. They came back to see "Black Mac" (Father Charles McCarragher, who ran a tight ship in the dorm and patrolled the bars at night). They came back to see the "Sneakin' Deacon" (Father Paul Fryberger, who legend claims ran down the dorm corridor to quiet a party with one shoe and one sneaker so that he seemed to be walking along slowly). Alums come back in gratitude for those men and women who lived with them in their residence halls and dealt with their first mistakes in a way that led them to grow up.

When they were adolescent in their behavior and found themselves in trouble or at times even in jail, the personal care they then received stayed with them forever. Youth and inexperience are not an excuse for wrongdoing, but the mistakes of youth do remain understandable. The Notre Dame campus is a great place for a party on Saint Patrick's Day and a great place to learn, with some help, how to be responsible for one's choices and indeed the outcome of one's whole life. Bishop Saint Patrick would understand and approve.

Stations of the
Cross: Lent

ON THE TUESDAY of Holy Week, hundreds of students at Notre Dame follow the way of the cross set across the whole campus. With lighted candles they gather in the evening hours in the Grotto to begin the fourteen Stations of the Cross. The procession winds around many buildings of the campus, with a station at places where the large crowd can readily assemble. Readings and reflections put together by a residence hall or some consolidation of volunteers are recited. Song and prayer are interwoven. The candlelit procession moves on from the steps of the School of Architecture, down the east–west quad in front of the South Dining Hall, to the reflecting pool of the library, where the mural of Jesus dominates the night scene, to end eventually in the Basilica of the Sacred Heart, where the last station is recited and a Lenten penance service concludes the evening.

Throughout Lent the Stations of the Cross are prayed in the Basilica on Friday evenings. People from campus and from town are faithful in attendance, and a procession of candle bearers and cross stops by each of the large paintings depicting the scenes of the way to Calvary. A prayer follows, then a reflection is read, and a song intervenes between stations. On Good Friday the Sacred Heart parish community prays the outdoor Stations of the Cross and winds around the southwest edge of Saint Joseph's Lake and then climbs the long hill to the life-size crucifixion scene in the woods nearby the old Moreau Seminary (now the Parish Center of the Sacred Heart Parish that worships in the crypt of the Basilica).

Every chapel in the twenty-plus residence halls on the campus displays the Stations of the Cross. As a popular private devotion, its day may have somewhat declined, but the mystery of the cross is yet depicted on the walls for those who can read the handwriting. Every classroom in the university displays a small crucifix in plain sight, and its presence there is deliberate. In that strange and even originally obscene symbol, we see ourselves and our world. We see what we do to each other, what we do to ourselves, and what others do to us. Humanity has lived a violent history. We take life as well as give life. The cross remains the mystery of God's love for humanity in the death of Jesus, the son of God become man who gave himself for us. "This is my body, given for you." In such sacrificial love is the hope of the world, for love is stronger than death. The motto of the Congregation of Holy Cross, founders of Notre Dame University, is *crux, spes unica* (the cross, our only hope). Those words are symbolized by a cross with an anchor as a background. Only the cross can anchor our life in God amid the storms of this life.

Of all the stations, surely the legendary story of Veronica[4] is the most intriguing of them all. She is a figure of mystery, emerging out of the crowd and then disappearing, taking with her the one and only likeness of Jesus miraculously imprinted on the cloth with which she wiped the blood, sweat, and tears from his face. Who was she? Any one of us ought to have stepped forward and rendered this simple kindness to this gentle man helpless and in such obvious anguish. But it is told that only Veronica stood up for Jesus with a cloth in her hand and no mind to the consequence. One should never be a mere spectator to agony. "Random kindness and senseless acts of beauty" confirm our humanity. Compassion is ever like the princess who kisses the frog, ever like the beauty that embraces the beast, ever like the love that is willing to touch the leper's pain and turn it into blessing. It is when Veronica covers the disfigured face of Jesus that she discovers the divine face of her Lord and savior. So ought we all live—students, faculty, and staff of Notre Dame.

Compassion arises because people love one another, and compassion reflects the love of Christ for the world. His image should be imprinted not only on the cloth but also on our hearts. We should live as human beings made in the image of God with his love seen on our faces. "The thirst for

---

4. In the legends of Veronica, she is thought to be the woman with the hemorrhage, who touched the clothes of Jesus. "Who touched my clothes?" asks Jesus (Mk 5:30). "He looked all around to see who had done it. But the woman, knowing what had happened to her, came in fear and trembling, fell down before him, and told him the whole truth" (Mk 5:32–33). The man whose cloth had stopped the woman's bleeding of twelve years' duration now suffers his own flow of blood, which she arrests a moment with her cloth touched to his face.

communion is evoked every time I look at Veronica's veil with the face of Christ on it and the face of all whom I love" (Henri Nouwen). The woman who gives Jesus to drink at the well; the woman who washes his feet with her tears and dries them with her hair; Martha, who feeds Jesus; Mary, who sits at his feet to listen; and Mary Magdalene, who comes to the tomb with spices to anoint his dead body—these are the Veronicas all over the world who show the face of Christ. They offer peace, not war; hope, not despair; life, not death; gratitude, not resentment; forgiveness, not revenge; mercy and not pain. Veronica is a moment of sanctuary for Jesus, a moment of being at home in a woman's arms, where all life begins and where it so often ends.[5] Mary, the mother of Jesus, wrapped him when a baby in swaddling clothes and laid him in a manger, and she who stood at the foot of his cross surely wrapped his body in the linen burial cloths and laid him in the tomb "in which no one had ever before laid" (Jn 19:41).

Notre Dame students often encounter death for the first time during their college years. Many of our students have never been to a funeral. The death of a grandparent or of a father or mother can be a moment of truth and a moment of anguish. The death of a Notre Dame student saddens the whole campus and can traumatize friends and roommates. The Notre Dame family never appears more genuine than at these times, when the people of Notre Dame rally to the support of those who mourn. We hope always to recognize one another at our own station of the cross—in this place, at this time.

---

5. Much of the material about Veronica is taken from my book *Where Joy and Sorrow Meet* (Notre Dame, Ind.: Ave Maria Press, 1998), 78–81.

Saint Joseph: March 19

MOST OF US have entertained ourselves with jigsaw puzzles. Devotees seek puzzles with a thousand pieces and even with minimal pictorial detail, all of which make the puzzle more of a challenge. Many of us have worked smaller puzzles with a beautiful picture of the finished puzzle on the cover of the box. We know what the puzzle will look like when completed. Imagine that our lives and the life of the whole world could be compared to a puzzle of countless events and episodes. These pieces of our life story or the larger world story are given to us in episodic fashion, one piece at a time. We may have been working on a corner of the puzzle where all the blue-colored pieces belong. Suddenly we are given a red piece, and we have not the slightest idea where that piece belongs. We might be tempted to think we do not need it or it does not fit in. But what we are given in our life belongs to the full picture of our life before God, and we have to be willing to accept the providence of God that places each and every moment in the complete picture, knowing that the beauty of the final fulfillment justifies whatever the color and shape of the individual moment. Similarly, we may have worked the corner with the blue pieces but found we are missing one. It would be so easy to fit it in, but we cannot find that piece in the jumble of unplaced pieces that surrounds us. We need to believe that piece will be given us in due time. Whatever pieces of life are given us belong in the picture of God's providence, and whatever belongs in the picture of God's love for us will be given us. The pieces all fit, and they shall all belong.

Joseph of Nazareth did not know how the piece about the pregnancy of Mary, whom he had not yet married, fit in. But he believed it did fit in God's providence, and he was obedient to God's will that he take Mary as his wife and raise Jesus as his child. The Joseph in the story of the book of Genesis did not know how the episode of his being sold into Egyptian slavery by his own brothers would fit into the picture of the salvation of Israel. But that piece did belong to the whole unfolding of the history of the people of God and the promised land. Joseph had to be enslaved in Egypt so that he could rise by God's providence to a position of prominence in Pharaoh's court. Thence only could he ensure grain for his brothers in their time of famine. When his brothers, who betrayed him, feared reprisal from Joseph, he explained to them, "Do not be afraid! Am I in the place of God? Even though you intended to do harm to me, God intended it for good, in order to preserve a numerous people, as he is doing today. So have no fear; I myself will provide for you and your little ones" (Gn 50:19–21).

A statue of Saint Joseph can be found in most Catholic churches—usually on the right-hand side of the congregation, in plain view, and balanced by a statue of Mary on the other side of the sanctuary. At Notre Dame, Saint Joseph holds a place of honor in the Basilica. A prominent fresco depicts

Joseph in his last hour, with Mary and Jesus at his bedside. Death was sudden and frequent for the early builders of Notre Dame. Epidemic illness struck more than once. Joseph was the patron saint of a Christian death and the patron saint of manual laborers. The large statue to Saint Joseph, standing just east of the original Notre Dame college building, is a monument to his virtuous integrity and loyal service. Father Edward Sorin, C.S.C., founded the University of Notre Dame, but the lay brothers of Holy Cross built the university, and without them the founder would have foundered. Their patron was Saint Joseph, the laboring carpenter, the husband of Mary and the foster father and guardian of Jesus, the man of faith in divine providence. Such faith goes back a long way in the history of Notre Dame.

Every year after the return to campus from spring break and about the time of the feast day of Saint Joseph in March, the largest basketball tournament in the world commences at the University of Notre Dame. More than 500 teams are formed. Students play alongside faculty and staff members. The president of the university joins a team, and the football coach as well. Varsity athletes play with rank amateurs. Women and men play on the same team. Some teams have not a prayer, but they play to join the party. Some clown on the court, and others play with razzle-dazzle. Height and weight count, but fast and sharp count even more in this streetwise basketball on asphalt courts, whatever the weather: rain or snow. Only one varsity athlete per team is allowed, but the occasional unknown perimeter shooter makes you wonder if he (or she) should not be a walk-on for the varsity. They name themselves, and some team names are hilarious and others so "colorful" they are censored. Elimination competition halves the number of teams quickly. At the end a final four emerge, and then there are only two. The winning team is likely not the biggest or the most talented, but the one with the indomitable heart, artful strategy, and deadly shooting. Teamwork will win the day. The competition is democratic. The whole campus is involved. At times there are rivalries along the lines of race or residence. The courtside commentary can be as cruel as the pavement is hard. But in the end, the Notre Dame campus has pulled together, either as player or fan. Bookstore basketball, so named because the courts used to be behind the old bookstore by Badin Hall, is a spring ritual at Notre Dame. New basketball courts have been built behind the new Hammes Bookstore on Notre Dame Avenue. The legend lives on. It may be the first real teamwork asked of incoming students. If Saint Joseph was a master carpenter, he would have appreciated the precision and coordination of body and mind required to make a basketball team smooth. Were Joseph of Nazareth here, I think he would have played himself and taught Jesus how to play, and Mary, too. It's a family thing. We all belong, and all the pieces of our days belong to God's providential plan for our own welfare.

The Annunciation of the Incarnation: March 25

THE CHURCH BELLS of Notre Dame remain accustomed sounds on the campus. One hardly needs to look at the clock on the four sides of the belfry to tell the time. One need but listen to the music of the passing of the hours tolled by the bells—one light stroke for fifteen minutes after the hour, two for the half hour, three for the next quarter, and four for the hour, when a larger and deeper bell strikes the number of the hours of the day. When I was an undergraduate student at Notre Dame and enrolled in the Navy ROTC, I learned the pattern of ship's bells that told the hour of the watch so that all on board knew their duty. Time and eternity crisscross in the steeple belfry of the Basilica of the Sacred Heart, and the sounds of the bells remind us of our home in eternity.

I live in Corby Hall, next door to the bells of the Basilica. Twice a day the bells announce the Angelus,[6] which still

6. Three bells three times make up the Angelus, a medieval prayer form that speaks of the angel (angelus in Latin) Gabriel, who came to a humble maiden in Nazareth whose name was

sounds the good news of the incarnation of God's son, the Word made flesh, who even now dwells among us. At noon and at six in the evening, the bells ring the Angelus right before the hour is struck.[7] Most of the campus probably does not know that the Angelus owes its origin as a Christian devotion to Saint Francis of Assisi. Lamenting the sad state of affairs between Muslims and Christians in his day (as in ours), Francis set out to visit the Muslim sultan of Egypt in a gesture of reconciliation. He was cordially received, and when he returned to Italy, he brought with him a great respect for the Muslim call to prayer proclaimed from the minaret of the mosques several times a day. Christians, thought Francis, should also be called to prayer—morning, noon, and night. The Divine Office was traditionally prayed throughout the day and night by monks and canons of the Church, but laypersons were not called to prayer in a regulated way. Ordinary people in the city and the fields should be encouraged to stop whatever they were doing and pray with the Mother of God her words, as found in Luke's Gospel, upon the overshadowing of the Holy

---

Mary. The prayer goes, "The angel of the Lord declared unto Mary, and she conceived of the Holy Ghost. Hail Mary. . . . Behold the handmaid of the Lord; be it done unto me according to thy Word. Hail Mary. . . . And the Word was made flesh and dwelt among us. Hail Mary. . . ." The bells ring rapidly, and I can say only the medieval Hail Mary that ends with "the fruit of thy womb, Jesus" for each three-bell cadence. Then one says during the subsequent nine bells, "Pour forth we beseech thee, O Lord, thy grace into our hearts, that we to whom the incarnation of Christ thy son was made known by the message of an angel may by his passion and cross be brought to the glory of his resurrection through the same Christ Our Lord. Amen."

7. The Angelus at six o'clock in the morning has been found too early for a sleeping campus.

Spirit that centers the whole world in Jesus Christ, the Word of God made flesh in her.

During funerals in the Basilica, the largest and deepest bell in the belfry is tolled in single strokes spaced far apart in mournful sound. After a member of the Holy Cross community has died on campus, the bell is tolled in similar fashion. The tolled bell calls us to pray for the dying and the dead in their passage from time to eternity. The tolled bell calls us to ask who has died. Is it one of our own Congregation of Holy Cross, or is it a scheduled funeral in the Basilica? The time of day is a clue, but only that. Whenever the bell tolls, our prayer should also include the living in this reminder of that most crucial moment of our life when we meet God in eternity. John Donne had it right: "Never send to know for whom the bell tolls; It tolls for *thee*."[8]

When I lived in Moreau Seminary on the northern edge of the campus, one of us was given the job of ringing a handbell in the corridors of our residence to wake us from sleep to begin our day and to call us to morning meditation and prayer. The bell called us to the very regulated life we led in monastic community striving "to know, to love, and to serve God in this life and to be happy with him forever in the next" (from the *Baltimore Catechism* text folks my age learned as children). The bell ringer was called the "regulator," and the bell was called "the voice of God." The bell called us to do God's will. The bell reminded us of God's call in our lives to prayer, to community, and to the labors of the day. No moment of the day was left ungraced. Everything was done by the will of God and in obedience to the superior of the

---

8. John Donne, *Meditation XVII.*

community, whose will we embraced as God's will for us (unless what was commanded was sinful). We listened for the voice of God. As Eli said to Samuel, "When you hear the voice in the night again, say, 'Speak, Lord, for your servant is listening'" (1 Sm 3:9).

The bells of Sacred Heart Basilica call the campus to prayer. They announce the beginning and the ending of liturgical ceremonies within its walls. The bells that strike the hour and punctuate the day with regularity call us all on this campus to remember the Word of God made flesh in a stable of Bethlehem. When Gabriel announced to Mary she was to be the Mother of God, the world stood still and time stopped a moment. No other event in all of time can boast of such an intersection with eternity. And when she said, "Be it done unto me according to your word," all time was divided forever between before Christ (B.C.) and after Christ (A.D., anno Domini, i.e., in the year of the Lord). The God who was born in the manger now lives in the marketplace and walks on the campus. We are the body of Christ. We are his hands and his feet, his heart and his compassion for suffering humankind. One of the revered priests of yesteryear in the Congregation of Holy Cross used to say that he never turned down an invitation when asked to speak or serve in some capacity on campus. He would say this: "How else would God ask us to do something but through the voice of another human being?" Here is an incarnational spirituality, a most Catholic way of life. The bells of the campus steeple topped with the gold cross but reinforce the good news. The voices we hear with our ears proclaim the presence of God, and the invitation of the pealing bells reminds us that God speaks if we but listen and follow with our lives.

Holy Week: April

HOLY WEEK begins with the Palm Sunday entrance into the holy city, Jerusalem, and it ends with the resurrection of Jesus from the grave on Easter Sunday. The Last Supper of Holy Thursday and the crucifixion of Jesus on Good Friday tell the gospel story in its essence. "Jesus loved his own [i.e., all of us] to the end" (Jn 13:1). These Holy Week liturgies that present the paschal mystery in solemn remembrance and sacramental presence reveal worship at Notre Dame in its most elaborate effort to celebrate in some proportionate way the events of God's love for the world in the death and resurrection of his Son. One can go to Saint Peter's in Rome, or to the National Cathedral in Washington, D.C., or Westminster Cathedral in England, or anywhere else around the world and not find liturgy done with such loving devotion to detail and with such extraordinary resources. Notre Dame enjoys both a school of liturgy and a school of music. The student choirs at Notre Dame are many, and they are talented voices well trained and conducted by musically creative directors. The Basilica staff members know what high-church liturgy is all about, and the restored Basilica shines in its original architecture and its contemporary embellishment. Nothing within God's house but the best. Nothing unrepaired or unclean. Sacred space deserves the very best materials, design, and creative decoration. Imagine multiple choirs of students devoted to music and to their faith, a liturgy well designed and rehearsed in a setting as glorious as human resources can ensure and set in the presence of a standing-room-only congregation eager to be there and to enter into the holy mysteries, and one has a small idea of the solemn grandeur of Holy Week liturgy at the University of Notre Dame. I do not think it is done any better anywhere else in the world, though of course I have not been everywhere.

Except for the student choirs and servers, except for the students to be baptized at the Easter Vigil and their sponsors, except for a very few students who remain at Notre Dame over the Easter holiday or who bring their families here to worship with them in these days, the student body at Notre Dame is away and misses this week of weeks in the spiritual life of the university. I wish we could arrange that our students would stay for this week of superb liturgy and prayer at least once in their years at Notre Dame. On their college campus and with their alma mater, let them be part of this sacred week, which remembers the events that changed the world into a new creation. Death was overcome for humanity, and the meaning of suffering ever given hope that the love of God includes our every tear, even while we await a world promised and to come, when "God will wipe away every tear from their eyes" (Rv 7:17). Let them begin with the procession that follows the crossbearer from the steps of Bond Hall (the old Notre Dame library) into the Basilica on Palm Sunday morning. Let them attend by candlelight the midnight Holy Week Tenebrae services, which mark the ancient practice of the Church keeping prayer vigil even by night. Let them see Jesus in the priest washing the feet of the men and women assembled in the sanctuary of our campus church. It is an example of what we should be doing every day for one another since our Lord and Master came to serve and not be served. Let them pray the Stations of the Cross during the three hours of Good Friday when Jesus hung on the cross, and then let us all listen to the Passion story presented with song and instrument so that our hearts may also be kindled. Let us come on Good Friday to kiss the cross of Christ with a fraction of the love with which he bore it for us. Let our students see their own fellow students come to the baptismal font and recite the Apostles' Creed at their sacramental initiation into the Church during the Easter Vigil in the dark before Easter morning. And then may they come again to God's house for Easter Sunday evening vespers with prayer, with candles lit from the sole Paschal candle, and be sprinkled with Easter baptismal waters. One might well make pilgrimage to Notre Dame for Holy Week.

Let me not imply that less elaborate liturgies are less worthy, or that the way of amazing grace may not be found in humble places. God is well served in plain liturgy with limited resources. Holy Week celebrated at home with family and friends needs no apology. I do not promote high liturgy everywhere and all the time. And yet I dream of our students having seen heartfelt extravagance so that they will bring a hopeful heart and a more experienced eye to whatever place and whatever quality of liturgy they encounter. Let them know what it is to lavish, and they will be more ready and able to contribute in their own homeland.

Perhaps my dream of Holy Week at Notre Dame for all our students may soon be more than a dream. Sunday morning mass throughout the year is now being televised to a national audience. The cameras are small and well hidden, and they are operated by remote control from a central room in the basement of the Basilica. At first the televised mass may seem an imposition that makes the liturgy something of a performance. I have felt awkward knowing that the camera may find me distracted in the congregation or among the concelebrants. The need to stay within the hour of televised time pressures the celebrant and the homilist to be mindful of the ceremony clock, whose discrete display faces them. And yet, to invite a million viewers to pray along with the faithful of Notre Dame is a service and a privilege. Our students who each year find themselves at home for Easter with friends and family may finally come to know something of Holy Week at Notre Dame. It would be a dream fulfilled to worship together on these holy days as the holy family we were meant by God to be. We would have the whole world gather at one altar, but any one church building can embrace only a limited number of people. Hence the many churches in many places. On this week of weeks, during this holiest of weeks, how wonderful were we all to join minds and hearts by the miracle of technological communication and celebrate Holy Week together at least the one time as one campus community—friends, students, alums, faculty, employees—all the world.

Ordination Day: After Easter

THE SATURDAY after Easter has become the traditional day for celebration of the sacrament of Holy Orders at the University of Notre Dame. On this day Holy Cross seminarians who have just finished their Master of Divinity program are ordained to the priesthood in the Basilica of the Sacred Heart. For many years priesthood ordinations on the campus took place on the feast day of the birth of John the Baptist (June 24). There was a reason for that date. Jesus was in all likelihood apprenticed to John the Baptist. In the baptism at the river Jordan, Jesus became a disciple of John. He learned to preach from hearing John. Jesus had been a carpenter in Nazareth, and he had no experience as an itinerant preacher and a baptist. He must have been impressed with the holiness and the ascetic demands of John's message: "Repent, for the kingdom of heaven has come" (Mt 3:2). One might say Jesus spent his college education and his seminary years with the mentoring of John the Baptist. Later we read in John's Gospel that Jesus was sent by John into Judea to baptize (Jn 3:22–24). In the end, when John was imprisoned and subsequently beheaded because he told King Herod it was wrong to take his own brother's wife (Mk 6:18), Jesus took up the mission of John and the mission of baptizing in Galilee itself. No doubt Jesus knew that what happened to John and all the prophets before might well happen to him. Jesus soon discovered that he could do more than John, who would only scold and could not change the hearts of men and women. The baptism of John was only one of water, which rolled off the skin and could not cleanse the heart. Jesus did more than scold. Jesus touched hearts from within. He baptized with fire and the Holy Spirit. Jesus could enable people to change their lives because his words illumined their minds and his touch enkindled their hearts.

Jesus called disciples to be apprenticed to his ministry in the care of souls. Today that call is still heard and still answered. Of fourteen children of a family in Huntington, the heartland of Indiana and the home of the old Catholic newspaper *Our Sunday Visitor*, Tom was the last one. As I write this paragraph in 2003, he was ordained a priest in the Basilica at Notre Dame. In a media interview, his mother said this:

> Tommy would always get rid of things: in seventh grade, then high school, and again in college. He gave some real nice clothes to his nephews. He always wanted to go to other countries to be with the poor, and he did go to Chile [as a seminarian]. He was a senior in college when he phoned me to say he was going to Moreau. I asked him, "What country is that in?" You could have bowled me over with a feather. I broke into tears I was so happy. . . . The kids tell me when he was born, I said something like, 'This one is for God,' but I don't remember. That's up to the Lord. We just pray that he keeps on the path he's on

now. We pray for perseverance. He just loves what he is doing.

Celebrating sixty years as a priest, Father Theodore Hesburgh, C.S.C., in a media interview at this same time, said this:

> I never wanted to be anything but a priest. I've celebrated more Masses than I've had days as a priest. I've offered Mass at 50,000 feet in the air, on a submarine 700 feet under the ocean, and on an operating table at the South Pole. Celebrating Mass every day is what makes me most conscious of being a priest. And a priest has to be faithful to a regimen of prayer. . . . If you're a priest, you belong to everybody. I wouldn't want to marry, even if I could, simply because my attentions would be divided. As a priest I can give of myself as Christ's life was given wholly to others. I've always believed I should be at the beck and call of anyone who needs my help. You always have to be aware that you're a servant and shouldn't be put out when people exercise their franchise with you. After more than fifty years on a college campus, I feel most at home with college students, but no one is exempt from my care, regardless of age, religion, or culture.

But the day belongs even more to Father Tom than to Father Ted. I look up at the choir in the loft at the back of the Basilica. I see the puzzlement on the faces of the men and women who are watching someone their own young age, who is admired and respected, lay down his life to try to serve them as Jesus came to serve and not be served. It is a puzzle. It is amazing grace.

Catholics deep down understand what remains most fundamental about Christianity. The Word became flesh and dwelt among us. No longer were we to seek God by climbing a mountain and yearning to draw closer to a heaven far away from this sinful valley of human tears. No longer did one find God by fleeing the world in its unloveliness. God came down the mountain and was born in the stable and lay in the manger where the animals found their straw food. The Son of God became like us in all things but sin, and Jesus became for us the bread of life. With all our sinfulness, we are now the body of Christ, wounded but graced as well, taken up by whatever our vocation, blessed by the Holy Spirit, broken by the burdens of the day, but given as the ongoing care of Jesus for his people, for whom he willingly gave his life. Ordination is indeed incarnational, for the priesthood is the continuation of the ministry of Jesus.

In the ordination liturgy, I think the most poignant moment comes when all the attendant priests are invited to file by in line in order to lay hands on the heads of those to be ordained and to invoke the Holy Spirit upon them. The line of priests comprises old and young, sorrowful and joyful, the whole human story of sin and glory. Those to be ordained will be no different. They too will struggle with the vocation to follow Jesus even to the cross. We are not better nor are we worse than those who came before us and those who come behind us. We are all sinners saved by the blood of Jesus. We are all wounded healers. And, we are all beautiful in the eyes of God, ordained or not, male or female, young or old, sinful or sainted, because God sees in each one of us the body and soul of his beloved Son. Indeed, the Word became flesh and dwelt among us.

The Fisher Regatta: Late April

AS I AM WRITING this account of springtime on Saint Mary's Lake, it is the dead of winter. The lake is frozen solid, but one no longer sees traffic crossing it to Holy Cross Hall of yesteryear, now only a memory. On this morning, the fire department has its equipment on the shoreline, and I watch firefighters practicing a rescue. Saint Mary's Lake receives the warm water from Saint Joseph's Lake, and where the inlet empties from under the road to Saint Mary's College, the lake is never quite frozen enough for safe passage. The fire department practices saving the life of anyone who falls through the ice. It is reassuring to see the firefighters put one of their own into the icy water and then enact a rescue.

Saint Joseph's Lake used to freeze when I was a seminarian in the 1950s. We walked across it in the winter in a shortcut to our classes. No longer does the lake freeze, especially where the power plant returns the warm water of its steam system into the lake at either end. Perhaps the winters are not as cold as they were fifty years ago, or perhaps our memories exaggerate, as childhood memories magnify the size of our home backyard, which today seems unintimidating. It is hard to imagine what Notre Dame would be like without the twin lakes. In the early years of the university, the one lake (Notre Dame du Lac) was divided only by swampy land, which was filled in order to give relief from mosquito-borne epidemics. Springwater from the east end of Saint Joseph's Lake continues to drain into Saint Mary's Lake through a culvert and flows out the western end into a small stream that empties into the Saint Joseph River, which flows into Lake Michigan and then into the Atlantic Ocean. I am reminded that our campus is connected to the whole world.

"Arise, my love, my fair one, and come away; for now the winter is past, the rain is over and gone. The flowers appear on the earth; the time of singing has come, and the voice of the turtledove is heard in our land" (Sg 2:10–12). When winter is done and the ice has melted, the joyful rites of spring begin on campus. Everyone here suffers from cabin fever. We have been too long indoors. As the grass greens and the sun warms, the outdoor life of the campus springs up anew. A carnival weekend precedes the serious work of the study weekend before final exams are given in the early part of May. It is late April when the students allow themselves their last fling and take part in festivities called An Tostal (a Gaelic word for just such a spring festival in the Emerald Isle). All kinds of fun and silliness are generated by the imaginations of young men and women with energy to spare and vitality to spend. There are sack races and trampolines, clowns and puppet shows. There are mud-pit wrestling matches (spectators, beware), chariot races, and the climax game of the Bookstore basketball tournament (see the chapter about Saint Joseph above).

Early on Saturday morning of this wacky weekend, there is the annual Fisher Regatta[9] on Saint Mary's Lake. For weeks each of the contestant dorms has been proudly building a boat. Boats are made of scrap lumber floated by barrel drums, inner tubes, or buoyant plastic foam. Some boats resemble canoes, and the rowers are almost submerged. Other boats resemble floating palaces, two-story rafts with sofa on the upper deck, where the boat officers lounge while navigating at leisure. Paint and decorations display hall pride or prove the adage "With friends like these, who needs enemies." Students have as much fun and laughter building the boat as paddling it across the lake in what passes for competition. Ostensibly a race across the lake from north to south, the regatta draws a crowd to watch a circus on the water. The fire department, the Red Cross, and the rescue squad are all there for safety and proud display. With some showmanship, motorboats accompany each homemade boat in its fragile progress by paddle across the lake, lest it sink and be without rescue. Sink they do, with some regularity, or at the least they take on plenty of water. One imagines melted ice water on a day often cold and rainy, as April in Indiana can be. To just not sink and make the crossing is a moral victory. One needs to be able to swim. The Fisher Regatta is a campus spectacle, and the crowd onshore gets into the fun with grilled "brats" and all the trimmings of a picnic, rain or shine.

Long ago we the living emerged from the sea. Before we were born, we swam in the salt water of our mother's womb. Our bodies are mostly water—warm water in a fragile envelope. I know how much our students love life itself, and I think that at the regatta they show love for their overall cam-

---

9. Fisher Hall sponsored the first regatta in the mid-1980s.

pus life. Most of all they enjoy each other in this farewell to the spring semester and in some ways the beginning of a farewell to their own innocence and their own childhood. One cannot sail the seas of Saint Mary's Lake forever, and some serious boating lies ahead for the graduates. Noah's Ark will no longer save humanity. It is the bark of Peter that now beckons the world to safe harbor. Jesus, who walked on the water of the Sea of Galilee and calmed the storms of this life, remains our hope to stay afloat. The nave of any Western church derives its name from the Latin word for boat (*navis*). The new church "ark" of the covenant floats paradoxically upside down on the heavens above. Those who board this boat must make adjustments and deal with mysteries. In this boat their bodies are buoyed up by the promise of eternal life. They will not perish in the storms of time. Baptismal robes are life preservers. Safe harbor is foreseen and seaworthiness guaranteed from on high. We sail together and God with us. If it takes imagination to build a homemade boat and a willingness to get wet to join in the Fisher Regatta, so it takes faith to walk into the nave of Christ's Church and a willingness to immerse oneself in the mature responsibilities of a Christian. This boat too must be rowed forward, and everyone needs to hang on to each other and take to heart the challenging words of Jesus: "Put out into the deep water and let down your nets for a catch" (Lk 5:4).

Final Exam Week: Mid-May

FINAL EXAMS SEEM so important to under-graduate students and so unimportant to me as a teacher. First-year students especially are anxious about their ability to compete with their classmates in a prestigious university where they are no longer big fish in a small pond set back in high school days. In the Great Books Program, where I teach, we give oral exams—two professors and one lonely student for thirty minutes. Some are comfortable with the live exchange, and others are just shy of petrified. I always give our first-year students in Great Books (who are sopho-mores) a rehearsal oral exam at midterm, and the exam does not count toward their grade. Then at least they have an inkling of what we are about in an oral exam. I tell them that the pro-fessors are not trying to find out what they do not know and so trap them. We are trying to find out what they do know, and if we ask a question that baffles them, they should say so, and we will go on to another question. No one can answer all questions, and I have sat in an oral final exam listening to the second professor asking the student a question that I could not well answer myself. So I tell them, we understand the nature of an oral exam. One of the professors was not the teacher of the course and hence might ask something about the text that never came up in class discussion. Such an oral exam is a very sobering experience. We start with the most general question. For example, what was the book about? According to the answer, a second question follows, and a third, each question perhaps more specific and in some ways more difficult to answer. The professors are being examined as well because one must, on the spur of the moment, come up with good questions that are fair, interesting, and answerable. We all sweat out an oral exam. The student who can stay with the questioning in an insightful manner unto the very end of the half hour will receive the highest grade. Even to know not the answer but only how to go about answering the question, had one world enough and time, is to excel.

Before final exam week, I always give my students a little talk on grades and exams. Teachers do not like to give grades any more than students want to be graded. Evaluation always seems arbitrary at some level, and none of us want to be judged when we believe no one understands the whole picture. I tell my students I would much rather write a letter of recommendation for every student at the end of the course. In that letter I would describe what I thought were the major strengths and weaknesses of the student as I have come to know him or her in this particular course. At graduation, one would have a folder of forty letters from one's teachers in four years of college work. Employers, however, do not want to spend time on so many letters. They want all the evaluation boiled down to one decimal figure, and believe it or not, some folks will conclude there is a significant difference between a 3.43 and a 3.51 average. I try to convince my students that there are only two distinguished grades—A and B. All minuses and pluses are shading of no consequence—at least in the liberal arts. A grade of C probably does not reflect a student's best efforts, and a D at Notre Dame stings like an F. There remains a difference between an A student and a B student. Beyond that I am skeptical, and I am quite convinced that a college grade average may enable one to gain that first job or opportunity, but afterward, one will be judged on current performance and not on past records.

In the small seminars that are taught in the Great Books Program at Notre Dame, the teachers have the luxury of knowing their students quite well. I have heard a student speak argumentatively many times, read numerous essays, and encountered the student outside the classroom often enough. I do not need a final exam to determine a grade. The students need a final exam, and the reason is that they need a review of the entire course. They need to consider the material we covered in the first week of class in the light of what we understood at the end of the course. If the students would promise to do the review, we could cancel the final exam. However, knowing human nature, I realize the final exam is the motivation to pursue a thorough review. Sonnets consist of fourteen lines for a reason. The mind can still remember the first line of a sonnet when reading the last line, but our memory cannot span much more than fourteen lines at one time. College courses are about fourteen weeks for the same reason. With a decent final exam review, one can comprehend in one configuration the material of the first week in light of the material of the last week. That done, class is dismissed.

One notices during final exam week a renewed devotion to the Grotto. Tradition has it that prayers at the Grotto can win a better grade on the final exam, especially if one has not studied and has come repentantly to the court of final appeal.

Surely the most compassionate Mother of God would understand such a predicament. And indeed Mary does console our students, pass or fail. Whether or not their grades improve upon prayer is not to be questioned. Peace of mind and less anxiety of heart will facilitate students' doing their best on a final exam. Memory will be clearer with prayer included in the exam preparation, and indeed I recommend a good night's rest as well and no foolish all-nighter to supplement an all-semester negligence. However, if one has studied very little and is asking for a miracle, that is possible, but I think not probable. The negligent student probably does not deserve one. Candles are lit, and prayers are never wasted.

Notre Dame students in large numbers study hard. We all hold our breath a bit during finals week. Campus ministry serves doughnuts at all times of the day and night. The dining hall and the library try their best to make the days friendly with ample hours. At the last, when in our oral exams in the Great Books course a student whiffs the soft-pitch question "What color was the whale?" we conclude he or she just did not get around to reading *Moby Dick*. That recognition is at least a minor tragedy. Perhaps another book, perhaps another question, perhaps even another day.

Graduation Day:
Mid-May

SENIOR WEEK fills the days between the end of final exams of the spring semester and the following Graduation Weekend. This campus has been home to the graduating seniors. For a long time, these residence halls have been home. These roommates and these friends—from classes, hall life, clubs, choirs, sports, and what have you—have become lifetime friends who shared for some years this home together. Good-byes are painful even when time is provided for the last days to linger in the heart. The last visits to the Basilica and to the Grotto give many students memories for a lifetime. A Basilica ceremony called "Collage of Word and Music to Celebrate Commencement," taken from the writings in the journals of senior-class members, concludes with the ancient Irish Blessing: "May the road rise ever to meet you. May the wind always be at your back. May the sun shine warm on your face. May the rain fall soft on your fields. And until we meet again, may God hold you in the palm of his hand." A candlelight procession to the Grotto follows with a musical setting of the words of

John Henry Cardinal Newman's poem "Lead, Kindly Light."
A last visit to Lake Michigan with a last beach party, or some
other evening reminiscence, brings nostalgic memories of all
the good times of college life, when one lives in the prime of
youth. Students at Notre Dame made deep bonds with
friends and sank roots in this campus. Many of these college
friends will stay in touch with each other from weddings to
funerals and everything in between.

Awards are given out on the Saturday before graduation,
when family and visitors have begun to assemble on campus.
The ROTC proudly commissions its graduating officers. The
many choirs of the university present recitals for the parents
and visitors. The Center for Social Concerns celebrates the
many graduates volunteering their lives after graduation with
a Service Send-Off Ceremony. The Phi Beta Kappa ceremony always moves me greatly as it folds together the early
days of this country and its struggle for political indepen-
dence with the years of struggle on the part of the best and
the brightest in higher education for intellectual indepen-
dence. To be inducted into this honor society, one must
achieve an integral education that is mindful of the complexity of truth and the excellence required in its pursuit.
The students are called by name and walk across the dais to
receive their membership certificates. With tears in my eyes,
I look for the ones I know, and I think if the future depends
on such wonderful men and women as these, the future is in
good hands. From them will come governors and judges,
teachers and newspaper editors, museum directors and doc-
tors. Just about any vocation is open to them. Their problem
will be an embarrassment of riches. So many choices; just
one precious life to live.

I love Graduation Day. I want to see the final product, the fruit of our labors, the children of our heart's and mind's involvement, the young men and young women at their best with their family and friends—proud, happy, and accomplished. I wish we could keep them with us. I feel like a parent whose children are leaving home. They will return to visit, but they had just matured as our equals and our friends, and now we must begin again with some persuasion and coercion to enliven the intellectual lives of the new-come students, sophomores all, who do not know how much they do not know. When I look at our seniors graduating from the Great Books Program at Notre Dame, I can remember their first days as sophomores with us. What a long way they have come. How a budding promise has bloomed to a rich, full personality with generous heart and judicious mind. One should be astonished. Like their families in the gallery around the graduation platform, I sit in the background and marvel at what the Lord has wrought. Perhaps time and vitality alone would have matured these students a great deal, and what the university has done does not deserve all the credit. Surely the antecedent education and parental influence and love of every kind claim most of the praise. Surely human nature and God's grace are behind whatever the efforts of the alma mater.

On Graduation Day I ponder how mysterious all human beings are and how little we know each other in that mystery of the human person whom only God knows. The ceremony of graduation nowadays allows time for only the doctoral candidates to receive their degrees by name and with a proud walk across the platform to accept the "sheepskin" diplomas in their hands. Many of these postgraduate men and women will educate the next generation of college students. The children of the undergraduates sitting beside them today may well know these doctoral graduates as their mentors in their education at their own alma mater—perhaps Notre Dame once again. In the roll-calling spaces of the graduation ceremony, I pray especially for our undergraduates whom I have known and whose presence I will miss. They have just begun their life's work. Several times in the graduation ceremonies, they are charged "to turn learning into service." Knowledge may be its own end in contemplation, but knowledge is also at the service of life in all its manifestations. At the last we shall all be judged on the charity in our hearts.

Commencement exercises are what we call the ceremonies of graduation. Now our students begin to channel that exuberance of erotic and irascible energies that, wisely employed, will result in lives of purpose, fulfillment, dedication, and service. The future belongs to this graduating generation. As they prosper, we will prosper. One can only bless them, celebrate their promise, hope with them and for them. We bring before them outstanding men and women who will receive honorary degrees, not necessarily for their academic work, but for their lives of learning already turned into service worthy of honor. Some of the honorary-degree[10] recipients have little formal education. Their talent was developed on the job and taught well in the school of life itself. Students fret over their transcript grades needlessly. Perhaps one's very first job is related in some way to one's academic record, but very soon no one cares about college scores. All will be judged on performance and on character. The credentials of life are virtues that we all recognize when we see them: goodness, competence, creativity, generosity, and dedication to truth and to compassionate humanity.

---

10. Father Theodore Hesburgh, C.S.C., president of Notre Dame for thirty-five years, holds the world record (as far as anyone knows) for the most honorary degrees given to one person—some 148 and counting.